Russia's Road to
Deeper Democracy

Russia's Road to Deeper Democracy

Tom Bjorkman

BROOKINGS INSTITUTION PRESS
Washington, D.C.

Library of Congress Cataloging-in-Publication data
Bjorkman, Tom.
  Russia's road to deeper democracy / Tom Bjorkman.
    p.   cm.
Includes bibliographical references and index.
  ISBN 081570898X (cloth : alk. paper)—
  ISBN 0-8157-0899-8 (pbk. : alk. paper)
  1. Russia (Federation)—Politics and government—1991- 2. Democracy—Russia
(Federation) 3. Democratization—Russia (Federation) 4. Elite (Social sciences)—
Russia (Federation) 5. Political leadership—Russia (Federation) 6. United
States—Foreign relations—Russia (Federation) 7. Russia (Federation)—Foreign
relations—United States. I. Title.
JN6695.B59 2003
320.947--dc21   2002155818

9 8 7 6 5 4 3 2 1

The paper used in this publication meets minimum requirements of the
American National Standard for Information Sciences—Permanence of Paper for
Printed Library Materials: ANSI Z39.48-1992.

Typeset in Minion

Composition by Oakland Street Publishing
Arlington, Virginia

Printed by R. R. Donnelley
Harrisonburg, Virginia

Contents

Foreword

Eleven years of dramatic change have slowly but steadily put Russia on a foreign policy course toward alignment with the West. Its movement toward a market economy is also plainly evident. But one huge uncertainty about Russia's future remains: the political order that will emerge to replace the highly authoritarian system inherited from the Soviet past.

In the first years after the collapse of the Soviet order, Western-style democracy was seen by many on both sides of the former iron curtain as a goal and a realistic possibility. During the 1990s, in the wake of political turmoil and economic hardship, the climate changed. Moscow's immediate goal became to reestablish political stability and rebuild the capacity of the state to provide essential services and implement government decisions across a country that encompasses eleven time zones. In the last years of former President Boris Yeltsin and the first years under President Vladimir Putin, this objective has meant adopting government policies that buttress the power of the president and the executive branch to execute the administration's policies. The Putin administration has also tried to constrain the chaotic pluralism that characterized the first post-Soviet years and sought to muffle opposition by creating a more compliant parliament and press.

The significance of these trends for the future of democracy in Russia inspires serious debate in Russia and the United States. Some see signs of the onset of a lengthy period of more authoritarian politics. Others see an intent to restore the capacity of the Russian state to execute policies, a necessary first step toward a strong and effective democracy.

In *Russia's Road to Deeper Democracy* Tom Bjorkman argues that the Putin administration's current policies are leading Russia toward a dead end. Only a renewed push toward deeper democracy, he says, will create the economic prosperity and global status that Russia seeks. He sees Russia's current course as being far less stable than it seems on the surface and the potential for political change far greater.

The data that Tom presents suggest that the Russian people are dissatisfied with the half-authoritarian, half-democratic institutions that have emerged in the post-Soviet era and are ready to support leadership in Moscow that takes action to build a deeper democracy.

Tom argues that America wields great influence in Russia, even more strongly after September 11 than before. The Bush administration can support and encourage an invigorated push toward deeper democracy in Russia not by lecturing Russians about their shortcomings but by placing democracy on the bilateral agenda and pursuing foreign policies that embrace Russia as part of the West.

On a personal note, I should add that I worked closely with Tom when I was in the State Department and he was at the CIA as research director for the Office of Russian and Eurasian Analysts, assistant national intelligence officer for the USSR, and in other positions in the Russia program. He and I were frequently together in meetings on how to deal with various issues that came up with the new independent states of the former Soviet Union. I regarded him as a superb intelligence officer and a fine public servant, so I've been delighted to have been able to work with him again during his stint at Brookings as a Federal Executive Fellow for the 2000–01 academic year. It gives me pleasure to see the Brookings imprint on his excellent book.

STROBE TALBOTT
President

March 2003
Washington, D.C.

Acknowledgments

I relied heavily on the work of the many Russian and Western scholars who have studied in depth the different facets of post-Soviet Russian politics and its still young democratic experiment. My suggestions for Russian and American policy draw on interviews with U.S. and Russian analysts and government officials. I owe these analysts, scholars, and officials a debt of gratitude for their original research and analytical opinions. I have sought to bring together in one place these many elements and to probe their implications for Russia's road to a deeper democracy.

I am grateful to the Central Intelligence Agency for the commitment it has shown to deepening the expertise of its officers through programs like the one that gave me the opportunity to spend the year at Brookings. While the CIA made it possible for me to write this book, the views I express are my own and are not intended to represent the positions of the CIA or the U.S. government.

I want to thank those who took time from their schedules to read part or all of this manuscript and offer me suggestions on how to make it better. I owe thanks in particular to Harley Balzer, Peter Clement, Cliff Gaddy, Jeff Hahn, Fiona Hill, Michael McFaul, Bruce Parrot, Bob Sharlet, Jim Steinberg, and the anonymous reader who contributed many fine ideas. I also thank Steve Grant and Keith Mosser for their expertise on opinion polling in Russia.

There could not be a better place to write a book such as this one than Brookings. The intellectual stimulation provided by resident fellows and diverse programs is liberating. The assistance I received from the library and other associates at Brookings was outstanding. At the Brookings Press, I owe thanks to, among others, Theresa Walker and Tanjam Jacobson for editing the manuscript, Caroltta Ribar for proofreading it, and Enid Zafran for preparing the index.

I would not have been able to complete this book without the assistance of Katherine Ballintine, who as a summer intern at Brookings demonstrated highly developed research skills and tireless energy. Finally, I want to thank my wife, Roxanne, who was reminded as I wrote this book that I have trouble focusing on more than one thing at a time.

Russia's Road to
Deeper Democracy

1

Democracy: Russia's Unfinished Business

In the fall of 2001 President Vladimir Putin decided to align Russia with the United States in a global war on terrorism. The invigorated U.S.-Russian relationship that followed has given new momentum to a formerly halting and uncertain post-Soviet march by Russia toward integration with the West. In the wake of September 11, few Western analysts now dispute that integration is the objective of President Putin and his team, even if the discomfort this objective has caused some of Russia's foreign policy elites is plainly evident.

Facilitating Russia's integration with the West holds the promise of contributing to American national interests and a more stable, peaceful, and prosperous world order. The Bush administration has recognized this potential and announced Russia's integration as an important goal of American foreign policy. Russian officials are already at work on the lengthy process of implementing policies and procedures needed to prepare Russia for entry into or closer cooperation with such organizations as the European Union and the World Trade Organization.

In the most fundamental sense, the factor that determines the pace and success of Russia's move toward integration will be the political order it builds on the ruins of communism. It is the virtual consensus of Western observers, and many in Russia too, that Russia's effort to build strong and vibrant democratic institutions in the decade since the Soviet collapse has stalled somewhere between democracy as understood in the West and the highly authoritarian order Russia inherited from the USSR. Imparting new momentum to Russia's movement toward deeper democracy will be critical to its integration with the West. A half-democratic Russia will at best be a half-ally of the United States.[1]

Why the Conventional Wisdom Is Wrong

Pessimism about the prospects for Russia's movement toward deeper democracy in the foreseeable future has become close to conventional wisdom. Many see recent steps by Russia's government to "manage" Russia's political institutions and place limits on opposition as a secular trend that is widely popular in the population and the elite, an understandable reaction to the political chaos and economic downturn associated with the tenure of former president Boris Yeltsin. Many would say that Russia is doomed to a period of semiauthoritarianism, and some would even accept it as a perhaps unpleasant but necessary stage in Russia's development.[2] In this book I present evidence that I believe shows that this conventional wisdom is far too pessimistic about the potential for political change and far too confident about the stability of the current half-democratic, half-authoritarian order.

Sizing Up the Current State of Russian Democracy

The political and societal leaders who started Russia's democratic revolution in the second half of the 1980s and the early 1990s disagreed on many things but shared a common conviction that Russia's future prosperity depended on a more pluralistic political order and more individual liberty. They would acknowledge that the revolution they began remains far from finished.[3]

Russian and American analysts vary widely in their assessments of Russia's success so far in building a democratic state, but much of this difference reflects the choice of different yardsticks with which to measure Russian reality. Some measure Russia in comparison to where it has been, while proponents of Western-style democracy measure Russia according to where they believe it still needs to go.

Viewed in the context of Russian history and the political reality of the USSR before Mikhail Gorbachev's election as Communist Party leader in March 1985, proponents of Russian democracy see substantial gains. Russian politics today is profoundly more pluralistic than before 1985. Competitive elections as the means to select leaders at all levels are common and widely accepted as the basis of legitimacy. Freedom of expression is dramatically expanded. U.S. government reports and assessments by nongovernmental organizations (NGOs) that track democracy issues in Russia agree that individual rights are better protected now than under the USSR. There has been some modest progress toward a rule of law that applies to the state as well as ordinary citizens, evident for instance in formal changes in the constitution and legal code and in citizens' increased resort to the court system.

In contrast, the reality of democracy in Russia falls far short when it is measured against the standards of established Western democracies and the aspirations of those prodemocracy political forces who brought down the communist system in 1991. Practice lags far behind Russia's success in creating formal democratic structures:

—Power remains concentrated in the executive branch, while legislative and judicial institutions remain too weak to create effective checks on the executive.

—More so than in established democracies, critical decisions are often made through corrupt relationships with government officials, informal networks, and personal connections to the president and his team rather than through formal democratic institutions and procedure.

—Economic hardship, the dependence of many institutions and individuals on state subsidies, and the lack of a robust "civil society"—that is, a network of nongovernment organizations able to put pressure on political leaders—leave individual liberties vulnerable to state intervention. Violations of civil liberties and state harassment of independent journalists and civic activists are on the rise since the late 1990s.

—Official corruption remains pervasive and the pace of movement toward a rule of law glacial.

Many observers characterize Russia as an "electoral democracy," emphasizing the degree to which the practice of multicandidate, competitive elections for choosing Russian leaders has gained greater purchase in Russia than have reliable guarantees of individual rights or a culture in which the rule of law holds sway. For many Russians, even those citizens who value greater freedom, the era of democracy has brought with it a lower standard of living, increased lawlessness, and a less just society. The practice of democracy varies widely across Russia's eleven time zones, and it is especially under challenge in some of Russia's eighty-nine regions where political parties, the idea of a separation of powers, and a free press are less well developed than in the large cities or at the national level.

Freedom House, a nonpartisan nongovernmental organization that measures and promotes democracy, provides the most systematic and widely accepted rating of the degree of democracy in Russia and other countries across the globe. The trend in the ratings Freedom House has assigned Russia since the mid-1980s is consistent with this summary of the strengths and shortcomings of Russia's progress toward democracy. Freedom House's panel of experts acknowledged significant gains in political rights, individual liberties, and rule of law in the last years of the Gorbachev era and the first years under President Yeltsin. But Freedom House figures describe a pattern of stagnation and even retreat from those advances since the mid-1990s. In recent reports, the organization dropped Russia's rating for political liberties on its seven-point scale from four to five, leaving Russia with a current rating of five for both political and civil liberties—at the low end of the category that Freedom House calls "partly free" (figures 1-1 and 1-2).

Thoughtful observers disagree on the reasons for Russia's failure to complete the construction of an effective democratic order in the ten years since the demise of the USSR. Some emphasize the legacy of seventy

Figure 1-1. *Measuring Russia's Democracy: Political Rights*[a]

Source: Freedom House, Annual Survey of Freedom House Ratings (www.freedomhouse.org).

a. The Annual Survey of Freedom Country Ratings classifies countries and territories as "free," "partly free," or "not free" by taking the average of their political rights and civil liberties ratings. On a scale from 1 to 7, 1 represents the most democratic. Countries ranking between 5.5 and 7 are considered not free.

Figure 1-2. *Measuring Russia's Democracy: Civil Liberties*

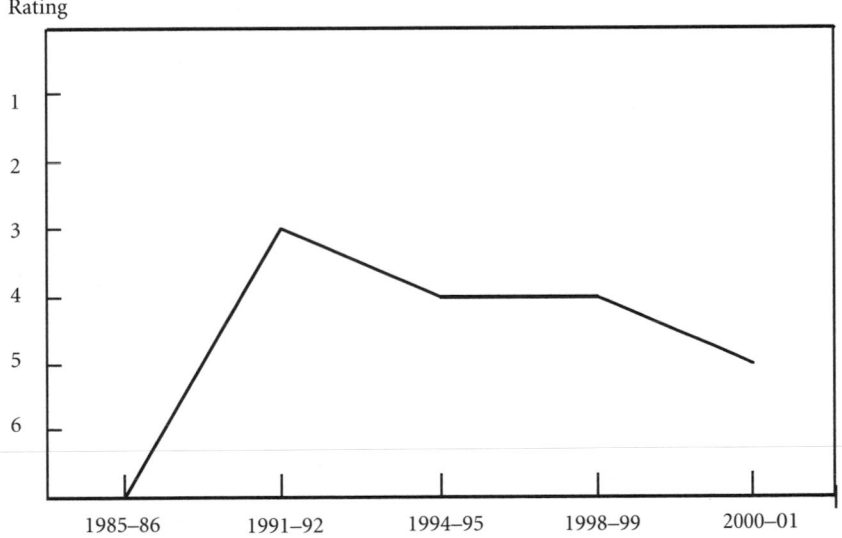

Source: See figure 1-1.

years of communist misrule. Others cite Russia's lack of historical experience with democratic values and behavior and the challenges of changing an inherited political culture. Still others emphasize leadership failures, especially Yeltsin's Byzantine, paternalistic style of rule and his failure to put priority on building viable institutions to fill the vacuum left by the collapse of communism. The evidence suggests that political habits inherited from the Soviet order, inexperience with the sometimes frustrating norms of democratic behavior, and leadership mistakes all contributed to current shortcomings.

The most important question for Russia today is not how to explain the past but how to chart a reliable path to deeper democracy in the future. More specifically, the challenge for proponents of Russian democracy is how to build support for a way forward in the immediate future, not in a vaguely defined "long term." In the long term, few if any would disagree that a stable and vigorous Russian democracy depends on a prosperous economy, the growth of a middle class determined to protect its private property rights, and a plethora of politically inclined and activist organizations in Russia's civil society willing and eager to hold its leaders to account. Few if any would disagree that over the longer term Russia's political future will follow a trajectory toward stronger democracy.

The Potential for Democratic Development in the Near Term

My focus is on the prospects for the near term—where there is more uncertainty and more debate about what to expect. There is more volatility in the current political environment in Russia than current headlines would suggest. There is more potential for change, in a democratic or antidemocratic direction. In this kind of environment, development of stronger democratic institutions in Russia is not guaranteed. But it is also not precluded. How this potential for change is realized will depend on political leadership in Russia and the West.

The factors that will determine the prospects for building stronger democratic institutions in the short term are different from those that will shape the longer term. In the short term, the potential for progress is less dependent on slowly changing structural factors such as economic prosperity and the size of the middle class and more dependent on current political attitudes, political leadership, and unforeseen political events. Measuring the potential for movement in a democratic or antidemocratic direction in the short term means paying close attention to the current spectrum of political opinion in the elite and society and in particular to assessing the support for current policies and the willingness to countenance political change. It means determining the degree to which Russians believe their current political institutions measure up to the kind of institutions they want and demand.

Russia is no longer a country where a handful of leaders at the top can for long dictate its political direction. A political course substantially out of alignment with political sentiments in society is a course that is unstable and subject to significant, and possibly sudden, change.

Popular Support for Democracy

Many analysts who are skeptical of the potential for movement toward stronger Russian democratic institutions in the near term base their conclusion on what they see as the prevalence of attitudes hostile to deeper democracy in Russian society. A systematic look at the results of professionally administered public opinion surveys—the best available data on popular attitudes in Russia—simply provides no support for the notion that popular attitudes are the cause of Russia's failure to move quickly toward stronger democratic institutions. These surveys are conducted by several of the serious Russian polling companies that have emerged in the past decade: the results of their research are published regularly in Russian print media and Internet websites.

Survey results suggest that support for values and institutions typically identified in the West with democracy is relatively low compared with support for those values expressed by publics in most Western democracies and even many developing democracies in eastern Europe and elsewhere around the globe. Substantial minorities express support for potentially antidemocratic policies, indicating that, after a decade of political instability and economic decline, there is less consensus in Russia about the kind of political order that should be built than there is in most mature democracies.

The more notable feature of these results, however, is that stable majorities have continued to express their view that democratic institutions and values are the right path for Russia despite the hardships that the past ten years have brought. Moreover, for the purpose of assessing support for democratic change, the most important measures are not the ones that compare Russian attitudes to those of publics in other countries but the ones that measure Russians' support for democratic values relative to the degree to which they believe their current institutions and government policies work to provide for and protect those values. On this scale, survey results show that Russians are highly critical of the shortcomings of their present democratic institutions and ready to back leaders who will push for stronger and more effective institutions.

There is simply no evidence to support the notion that Russians want more authoritarian institutions and much evidence to suggest they want change. Surveys show nostalgia for the Soviet era, but a closer look at these data indicate that the nostalgia is for the political stability and economic and social safety net that the USSR provided, not for its degree of political freedom.

Support for Democracy among Russian Elites

Some would say that, even if the public is willing to support democratic change, it is the opinion of Russia's elites that matters and Russia's elites are more antidemocratic than the Russian public. This argument understates the diversity in the political attitudes of Russia's elites and does not stand up to a systematic look at the results of widely available survey data on elite attitudes. Surveys of a representative cross section of Russia's political, business, and social elites indicate that, on the contrary, support for democratic values is consistently stronger among elites, sometimes much stronger, than among the Russian public. This result should not be surprising, since it is consistent with what opinion surveys show to be the case in many other countries.

Lessons learned from the experience of other countries facing the challenges of movement from an authoritarian order to a more democratic and pluralistic framework indicate that one of the greatest challenges is overcoming the resistance of the relatively narrow but entrenched segment of the elite that benefits from the existing order and stands to lose privileges in the open environment created by deeper democracy. The results of opinion surveys also suggest that in Russia too, it is not the public, or even the Russian elite as a whole, that stands in the way of democratic change in the near term but elements of the elite that are numerically small yet well positioned to impede political change. In this sense, a survey of societal attitudes in Russia suggests that latent support for democratic change in Russia is far more widespread than it seems on the surface and the defenders of the status quo far more isolated.

Everyone Favors Democracy, but What Kind?

As a theoretical concept, democracy faces no serious competitors in Russia today. The political debate has moved beyond the virulent divide between communists and "democrats" that prompted the political turbulence of the early and mid-1990s. Political figures that continue to suggest an ideological alternative to democracy no longer can gain much political traction ten years after the collapse of the communist order. Those who argue that Russia should seek some kind of special "third" or "Eurasian" way as an alternative to integration with the West seem to be in political decline. President Putin has said that there is no "third way" available.

But this considerable consensus on the idea of democracy and integration disguises fundamental differences in the elite about what kind of democracy should be constructed and in how much of a hurry Russia should be to construct it. Proponents of what some Russians call "managed democracy" subordinate democracy to the demands of rebuilding a strong Russian state. They appear to believe that building a strong state means a heavy hand for the state in deciding what kind of political development is necessary and in restricting the ability of any political opposition to assert a different point of view. In this environment, Russia's proponents of rapid movement toward Western-style civil liberties and restraints on the state—who make up a small minority in the parliament and other political institutions in the public political arena—are on the defensive. The policies of President Putin's administration have so far reflected this managed democracy mind-set, combining important steps toward a more liberal and market-oriented economic order with government policies that have erected boundaries on political expression and created new mechanisms for the state to control opposition.

The Potential for a Democratic Shift

Despite the seeming calm on the surface, many factors are coming together to produce a political environment ripe for change. The current contradictory mix of economic freedom and political authoritarianism will not produce the results that Russians are seeking. Although fortuitous factors have produced a period of solid economic growth in President Putin's first years, increasingly, economic success will depend on greater political transparency and a stronger rule of law that semidemocracy-semiauthoritarianism will not produce. The determination of Putin and his team to move Russia toward integration with the West and restore Russia's credibility as a major global player will run up against the barriers of "managed democracy." Pressures will grow for the leadership to move in a more resolutely democratic direction—or to further turn the screws on rising opposition. Putin's interests as president will begin to diverge from those of individuals who back authoritarian policies as he gets a stronger grip on power. These pressures will bring to the surface the divisions in the Russian elite and impel the broad swath of political leaders in the political center to get off the fence and take sides.

What Should a Democratically Inclined Leadership Do?

President Putin's position will be critical. So far he has spoken eloquently about democracy and even more so about integration with Western institutions, while presiding over an administration that has muffled political opposition and placed new strictures on political expression. He will need not only to come down more clearly in support of steps toward stronger democratic institutions but also to confront powerful constituencies in the federal bureaucracies and other vested interests who strongly oppose such steps. The pressures on him to do so will grow.

Confronting these powerful status quo constituencies will require far more than speeches or decrees. It will require mobilizing a coalition for change. The data I present suggest that there is a robust latent coalition for democratic change in Russia ready to be mobilized by strong leadership.

Should he choose to throw his weight behind a renewed push for democratic change, President Putin will find that Russia's proponents of deeper democracy have set out a sensible agenda appropriate to Russia's current conditions: key elements of that agenda include creating stronger checks on the executive branch, increasing the authorities of the parliament, building a more independent judiciary, creating a stronger, more competitive party system, stimulating democracy at the grass roots by enhancing the authority and the democratic character of local government, strengthening the structural foundations for an independent press, and building stronger guarantees for honest and transparent regional and national elections.

At the most fundamental level, the key to more vigorous economic and political growth is progress in reducing the power of entrenched elites, creating a more competitive political marketplace, and encouraging the development of a vigorous political opposition to those officials who are currently in charge. The single most important step that President Putin can take is to use his bully pulpit to encourage political opposition and throw the weight of the government behind steps that will expand rather than restrict the vigor of the political marketplace.

What Should America Do?

America's ability to support movement toward democracy in Russia and to deter movement in an authoritarian direction is substantial. Over the long term, government funding for programs that assist grassroots groups to develop a vigorous politically active civil society will be an important influence on the quality of Russian democracy. But in the short term U.S. diplomatic engagement can make a difference.

Supporting Russian democracy does not mean telling Russia what programs to implement. Even if the West had the answers, Russians would not listen. They are wary of Western advice about specific reforms and institutions, and the experience of the 1990s has reinforced the determination of Russia's leaders, from across the political spectrum, to seek indigenous solutions. America's most important contribution will be to create an international context that supports and stimulates those domestic forces seeking to move Russia in a more resolute democratic direction and that opposes and impedes domestic forces that are holding Russia back.

Studies of post-communist experience in the former USSR and eastern Europe show that the most powerful factor fueling democratic change in these countries has been the pull of the West and the opportunity to join Western institutions. When the potential benefits of "joining Europe" and becoming a part of the Western community of nations have been apparent, domestic forces pushing for democratic change have been strengthened, and policies promoting democratic values have been accelerated.

This experience suggests that policies in Washington that signal that Russia's integration into Western institutions is not just rhetoric but a core element of American strategy can change the political climate and undercut the proponents of "managed democracy," who are at the same time the most articulate skeptics of Russian policies that identify Russia's national interests as compatible with those of the West. Policies that signal that Russia's forthright movement toward democracy, an independent press, guarantees for human rights, and the rule of law is a vital concern for the United States will embolden Russia's proponents of democratic institutions and deter actions by Russian government agencies to harass political activists and repress political opposition. A convincing embrace of Russia's aspirations to join the West creates the necessary conditions for the United States to establish a dialogue at many levels with Russian leaders on the kind of policies than can encourage deeper democracy and hence faster integration with the West.

The desire of Russia's elite and citizenry to join the community of prosperous nations assures us that we have significant influence on how Russian democracy develops. The strategic reorientation toward the West prompted by September 11 only adds to U.S. influence and ability to carry on a dialogue about democracy in the context of cooperative relations. The history of U.S. diplomatic interaction with Russian leaders from Leonid Brezhnev through Putin suggests that U.S. engagement on issues of democracy and human rights has impact, even if that impact is not always immediately apparent.

Democracy in Russia Matters

Russia's development in a democratic direction is a vital national security concern to Russia and to the United States.

For Russia, studies of global development across many different countries suggest that democracy, with traits appropriate to Russia's history and conditions, is the most reliable way to build the strong and stable political institutions that all its citizens, across the political spectrum, desire. Democratic institutions produce strong states.[4] Faster progress toward deeper democracy, and the transparency that goes with it, is a proven way of reducing the hold of corrupt elites on the pinnacles of authority and unleashing individual initiative. Unleashing individual initiative is a necessary step toward the more just and prosperous society that Russians seek.

For the United States, Russia's development toward stronger democracy is a matter of practical national interest. The history of U.S. relations with established democracies suggests that a Russia with better-entrenched democratic institutions will be a more cooperative partner in the international arena, finding its national interests more compatible with American and Western interests than would a more authoritarian government. Proponents of stronger democracy and expanded individual liberties in Russia's domestic political debate are also proponents of Russia's full-scale integration into Western political and economic institutions.

On a day-to-day basis, Russian democracy does not need to compete with terrorism, security, or regional issues for equal time on the U.S. administration's agenda. But from a longer-term perspective, Russia's success in integrating into Western institutions and completing the transition to a strong, vibrant democratic state will be the most important factor creating the basis for a peaceful relationship and driving the United States and Russia toward a community of national interests. A substantial literature that examines the origins of war and peace during the past two centuries indicates that mature democracies do not resort to conflict to resolve their differences—a result of the sway of democratic norms for resolving conflict and the influence on state policy of those who would have to pay the price for conflict.[5] With the two countries edging toward greater consensus on security and regional issues, increasingly, democracy will loom large as an element of unfinished bilateral business.

Russia's success in building a more vibrant democracy will also have reverberations on the fate of efforts to construct democracy in the rest of the world. This is certainly the case with its neighbors in the political space of the former Soviet Union, where in many cases democratic progress remains as much under challenge—or more—as in Russia. Russia's success or failure in building a stronger democracy will pull its neighbors in the same direction. Students of global democracy see Russia as a "swing state" whose success or failure will have an impact on other countries across the globe whose efforts to build democracy are failing or stalled.[6]

2

Deep-Rooted Support for Democratic Values

The paradox is that Russian society is more prepared than its ruling class for deep transformations.

Russian political analyst Lilia Shevtsova[1]

Those who study global experience agree that the strongest and most effective democracies can typically be found in countries that exhibit a well-developed democratic political culture. A democratic political culture requires widespread support for democratic values and democratic habits of political behavior—such as tolerance of opposition and dissent and willingness to accommodate and compromise—that may be shaped by decades and even centuries of prior political history. No one should expect Russia to develop democratic institutions overnight as vigorous and effective as those structures in the most advanced democratic countries (box 2-1).

Russia's near-term agenda is not to develop institutions that look like those of the United States, the United Kingdom, or France but to chart a path that promises deliberate but steady progress toward more effective democratic institutions. To achieve this objective Russia does not require a society or a political culture that looks like the ones in the West. It needs instead widespread support among the elite—Russia's political,

Box 2-1. *Democratic Political Culture*

Students of political culture argue about the degree to which it is subject to change. Some historical studies suggest that cultural factors developed centuries ago can limit democratic development today. Other scholars say culture is dynamic and can change dramatically in as little as a generation. Some point to Germany, Italy, and Japan as examples of states that were said to be permanently antidemocratic and yet made successful transitions in a relatively short period. Studies of German political opinion indicate a sizable shift toward support for democratic values over the course of one generation following World War II. Many studies, looking at changes in political culture over longer periods, show a strong correlation between economic development and solidification of a democratic political culture.[1]

Douglass North, one of the most prominent students of institutional change, suggests that institutional change should be measured by changes in "culturally derived norms of behavior" rather than formal rules and political institutions. By this definition, institutional change in any society is overwhelmingly incremental. A seemingly discontinuous change, such as that wrought by the collapse of the Soviet Union and the establishment of a new constitution and formal political structures in Russia, is "seldom as discontinuous as it appears on the surface."[2]

1. The diversity of views about the significance of political culture and the constraints it places on a country's receptivity to democracy is displayed in the diverse views of the contributors to Lawrence E. Harrison and Samuel P. Huntington, eds., *Culture Matters: How Values Shape Human Progress* (Basic Books, 2000). Robert D. Putnam (with Robert Leonardi and Raffaeli Y. Nanetti) documents the influence on current democratic institutions of patterns of governance developed centuries ago in *Making Democracy Work: Civic Traditions in Modern Italy* (Princeton University Press, 1993). Larry Diamond discusses elements of a democratic political culture in Larry Diamond and Marc F. Plattner, eds., *The Global Resurgence of Democracy* (Johns Hopkins University Press, 1996), p. 119. Nicolai Petro points up the dangers of speaking about a "unitary" political culture in Russia in *The Rebirth of Russian Democracy* (Harvard University Press, 1995), esp. p. 19.

2. Douglass C. North, *Institutions, Institutional Change, and Economic Performance* (Cambridge University Press, 1990), esp. pp. 89–90.

economic, and social leaders—and the larger society for democratic values and a top leadership committed to building stronger democratic institutions. Such support does not need to be as widespread as in mature democracies, but it should be extensive enough to elect leaders who support stronger democracy and favor changing Russia's current institutions.

The most reliable data for weighing the depth of societal support for deeper democracy in Russia and measuring the potential for political change come from public opinion surveys. Anecdotal information about Russian attitudes must be taken into account, but public opinion polls offer the only systematic insight into popular attitudes across a spectrum of income, education, gender, and region of residence. Polls are also the only reliable insight into changes in the pattern of attitudes over time. The polling data tracking Russian public and elite views of democratic values since the late 1980s—when controls imposed by Soviet leaders began to collapse—until the present are extensive. There is a substantial academic literature interpreting those data.

Polling is an inexact science. With Russia's relatively brief experience with a pluralistic political order, questions remain about how ordinary Russians understand the meaning of democratic concepts and how willing they are to give answers they believe the interviewer may not want to hear. Some of the data are contradictory. By seizing on one particular question or choosing data selectively to fit a hypothesis, it is possible to support a variety of propositions about the flowering or withering of the democratic idea in Russia.

Despite these dangers, there is good reason to believe that survey data provide reliable insight into patterns and trends in societal attitudes during Russia's first post-Soviet decade. Many different polling organizations, drawing on surveys using different samples from different parts of the country and across different periods of time show consistent results. Typically, moreover, the differences in sentiment expressed by respondents in different categories of income, age, and education in Russia are consistent with what the differing responses to similar polls in other countries would lead one to expect.

Table 2-1. *Opinion on Democracy as a Political System*[a]

Percent

Country	Total agree	Strongly agree	Agree	Disagree	Strongly disagree	Don't know
Argentina	92	47	45	7	1	...
United States	92	49	43	7	1	...
Japan	92	19	73	8	1	...
Estonia	81	38	43	8	2	10
Georgia	77	27	50	11	2	10
Poland	68	23	45	8	1	23
Russia	59	10	49	35	6	...

Source: World Values Survey, Third Wave, 1995–98.

a. "Democracy may have problems but it's better than any other system."

The total of the vast array of survey research about Russian attitudes on democracy issues that has emerged during the past decade paints a coherent picture (table 2-1). It points to a society still subject to deep political divisions but one in which support for democratic values is stable and widespread. The data suggest eight propositions that sum up Russian attitudes about democracy and the development of democratic institutions:

—The Russian people want democratic institutions;

—Russians' first priority at present is "restoring order," but they do not equate order with authoritarianism;

—Support for democratic values is deeply rooted;

—Russians want to build democracy their own way;

—The Russian people are ready to back leaders who build stronger democratic institutions;

—Resistance to deeper democracy is centered in a small segment of Russia's political and economic elite, not in society and not in the elite as a whole;

—Russians blame the failures of the first post-Soviet decade on leadership failures, not on democracy; and

—Russia's leaders, not Russian society, must take the lead in building stronger democratic institutions.

Desire for Democratic Institutions

Opinion surveys that allow comparison of Russian attitudes toward democracy with those of publics in other countries show that support for democracy is disappointingly weak in that comparative context, and not just relative to mature democracies. Data from one such set of opinion surveys, the World Values Survey, show support for democracy in Russia ranking near the bottom of the countries included. The percentage of Russian citizens supporting the notion that democracy is the best system of government is lower than that in many developing countries as well as other countries of the former Soviet Union.

The relatively low levels of confidence that Russians express in democracy can be attributed partly to their dissatisfaction with the social and economic results of the past decade rather than to lack of support for democratic values such as civil liberties and free elections. But these data show that Russian history—especially the failure of Russia's first decade of democracy to produce significant progress toward a more just and prosperous society—have inhibited the development of consensus around the idea that democracy is the political system best suited to Russian conditions.

Despite this limited support for democracy in a comparative context, surveys show that support for democracy as the right kind of political system for Russia is widespread and has remained relatively stable over the first post-Soviet decade. Recent polls, for instance, show Russians strongly favoring democracy when they are given a chance to place their preference on a scale from full dictatorship to full democracy. Some survey results suggest that public support for democracy as a general idea grew during the 1990s, with larger numbers of Russians agreeing with the Churchillian statement that democracy is "the best possible system" despite its problems, and with fewer agreeing to the notion that democracies generate much talk but accomplish little. Other polls indicate that the proportion of Russians who say that they would actively oppose efforts to establish a dictatorship as a means to restore "order" increased during the mid-1990s (figure 2-1). Surveys show that, despite disillu-

Figure 2-1. *View on Dictatorship*[a]

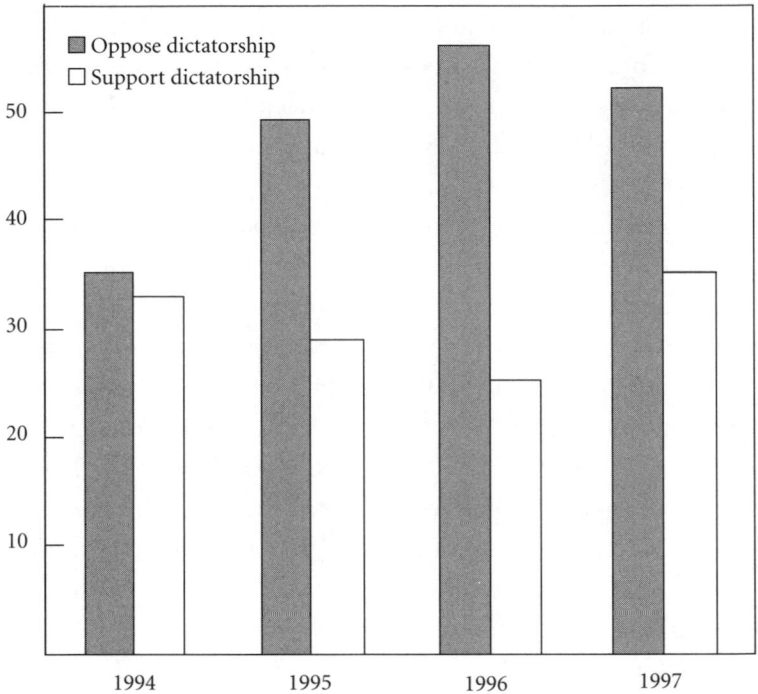

Source: U.S. Information Agency (USIA), Office of Research and Media Reaction, "How Unsteady Is Russian Democracy?" Opinion Analysis M-70-97 (May 1, 1997); and Richard B. Dobson, "Is Russia Turning the Corner? Changing Russian Public Opinion, 1991–1996," Research Report R-7-96 (USIA, Office of Research and Media Reaction, September 1996), p. 55.

a. "Some people say that restoring order is so important that they would support a leader who would use the military and the KGB to establish a dictatorship. Others say that freedom is so important that they would actively oppose any dictatorship. Which view is closer to your own?" Figure does not include "don't know" responses.

sionment with the effectiveness of their own post-Soviet institutions, most Russians disagree with the assertion that democracies are indecisive or that economies run poorly in democratic systems. [2]

Support for Specific Democratic Values

Opinion surveys that assess opinion about democracy as a general idea admittedly allow for many different definitions of democracy and could disguise significantly different levels of support for institutions and values associated with democracy as practiced in the United States and western Europe. Several polling organizations have tracked Russian opinion during the 1990s on specific democratic values and institutions such as freedom of expression and competitive elections, providing a potentially less ambiguous measure of the support for democratic values. The results of these surveys also show strong and continuing support during the 1990s for democratic institutions.

Elections

Survey data show steady support among the public for the idea that elections are the proper means to choose Russia's leaders and hold them accountable. Solid majorities of Russian citizens have consistently opposed canceling elections as a means to restore "order" in the country. In one 1999 poll conducted as speculation mounted about who would succeed former president Boris Yeltsin, 63 percent of Russians opposed canceling elections for this purpose, while 26 percent supported it. In other polls, large majorities of Russians chose "honest elections held regularly" as a feature of the society in which they want to live.[3]

Other data on election issues suggest that support for elections is more than an abstract idea. Surveys conducted well after the popular Vladimir Putin assumed power as president indicate that most Russians oppose steps either already taken or under discussion by the Putin administration that could be interpreted as reducing the role of elections in choosing Russian leaders. In polls in the fall of 2000, majorities opposed constitutional amendments that would allow the president to serve more than two terms or extend the president's term from four to seven years. In a May 2000 poll, majorities said that members of the parliament's upper house, the Federation Council, should be elected by popular vote rather than appointed by regional governors—the practice established following Putin's success in removing regional leaders as ex officio members of the council in the spring of that year. In an October 2000 survey, large majorities also said that the leaders of the eighty-nine regional entities that make up the Russian Federation should be elected by the people rather than named by the central authorities—another

Table 2-2. *Opinion on Mass Media*[a]

Percent

Respondents	Favor independent point of view	Favor authorities' point of view
All Russian public	55	27
Ages 18–24	62	22
Completed higher education	66	24

Source: All-Russian Center for the Study of Public Opinion (hereafter, Vtsiom) survey of public opinion, October 2000, published at www.polit.ru, November 28, 2000.

a. "Should mass media express views independent of authorities?"

idea that was reportedly being pushed by elements within the government at the time.[4]

Freedom of Expression

Polls consistently show that Russians support a free press and value their ability to speak their mind without fear of retribution. Survey results indicate specifically that majorities say the mass media should express an independent viewpoint, rather than the view of the government. For instance, in a July 2000 poll (table 2-2), more Russians said that mass media criticizing the policies of President Putin and the government were acting to the benefit of the nation (43 percent) than said that they were acting to its harm (30 percent).[5]

Majorities generally say they would oppose the imposition of state censorship as a means to restore order. Two separate polls in June 2000 and January 2001, in the wake of publicity over efforts by government agencies to harass the independent television channel NTV, indicated that more Russians say that the press is insufficiently free (33 percent in January) than say that there is too much press freedom (18 percent in January).[6] U.S. Information Agency (USIA)-sponsored polls on freedom of expression suggest that support for an open press may have solidified during the 1990s (figure 2-2).

Survey results show that many Russians who oppose state censorship and support the right of the press to speak freely are also willing to support state ownership of at least some media outlets and at least some

Figure 2-2. *Opinion on Censorship*[a]

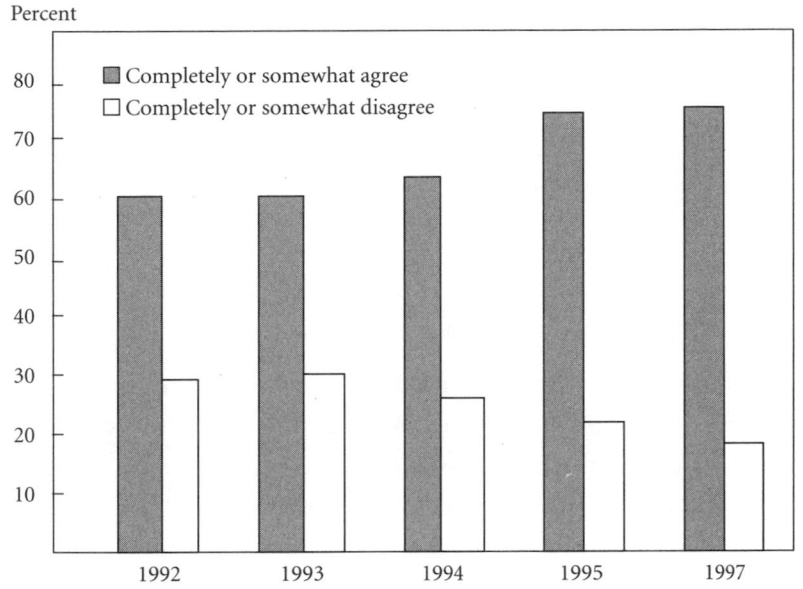

Percent

Source: See figure 2-1.

a. "People should be free to say whatever they want, even if what they say increases tensions in society."

controls over media content (see table 2-3). One November 2000 poll indicated that 38 percent of Russians said increased state control of the media would be beneficial, while 27 percent said it would be harmful. Some polls show that more Russians favor than oppose state control of national television channels. These results suggest that many Russians are dissatisfied with the way major media outlets were privatized in the 1990s—especially the success of a handful of prominent business leaders or so-called oligarchs in dominating major outlets—and more willing to trust the state than private interests as a guardian of the public interest. Some Russians also see state ownership as a way to control what they consider inappropriate sexual or other content. But the data clearly indicate that by supporting state involvement Russians do not mean to support state censorship or the suppression of dissonant points of view.[7]

Table 2-3. *State Ownership of Media*[a]

Percent

Ownership	1992	1993	1997	2001
State owned	62	75	76	73
Privately owned	27	19	19	18

Source: Department of State, Office of Research, "Russians Not Alarmed by Threats to Free Speech," Opinion Analysis M-2-02 (January 8, 2002).

a. "Should the mass media be state-owned or privately owned?"

Popular Support for Checks and Balances and a Separation of Powers

Historical experience has shown that as a practical matter democracy requires the creation of political institutions that protect those values by limiting the concentration of power and institutionalizing competition among different organs of government with independent bases of authority. Some authors have argued that one of the significant constraints on Russia's democratic development is a lack of a history or culture that supports creation of strong institutions separate from the executive that can constrain executive authority.[8] Survey data, however, indicate widespread public support for the commonsense notion that it is a bad idea to concentrate power in a single institution. Similarly, Russians support the idea that Russia needs a political opposition in the country prepared to oppose the course of those currently in power.

Various polling data suggest widespread recognition of the benefits of placing checks on the executive branch and distributing authority among ruling institutions. Separate surveys in different times have consistently shown that, when given a choice, most Russians would prefer to see power balanced between the president and the parliament rather than have it concentrated within the presidency or any other single institution (table 2-4).

A poll sponsored by the U.S. Information Agency in 1999 showed that 41 percent of Russians supported changes to reduce the current powers of the president, while 26 percent supported changes that would increase his authorities. Polling results show most Russians favor giving the par-

Table 2-4. *Distribution of Authority between the President and the Parliament*
Percent

Opinion of Russian public	1994	1999
President should be stronger/more important	25	21
Parliament should be stronger/more important	15	19
President and parliament should be equal in power	38	52
Difficult to answer	22	8

Source: Author's calculations based on results of similar but not identical surveys: 1994 data from Richard Rose and Christian Haerpfer, *New Russia Barometer III: The Results,* Studies in Public Policy 228 (University of Strathclyde, Centre for the Study of Public Policy, 1994), p. 38; and 1999 data from Timothy J. Colton and Michael McFaul, "Are Russians Undemocratic?" Working Paper 20 (Washington: Carnegie Endowment for International Peace, June 2001).

liament the power to confirm nominees for a wider selection of government posts than the handful provided for under the 1993 constitution and current legislation. Other polls show similar support for the idea that power should be balanced between the center and the regions rather than giving inordinate authority to either one.[9]

As with separation of powers, polling data indicate solid popular support for the idea that it is healthy for Russia to have a political opposition to officials currently in charge. USIA-sponsored polls in the early 1990s indicated that large majorities agreed that opposition is needed in a democracy. According to the results of one poll in the fall of 2000, despite the large majorities who express confidence in President Putin's leadership, 47 percent of Russians support (29 percent oppose) the idea that he needs an opposition. Respondents indicated support for the notion that such an opposition is necessary to exercise societal control over the leadership and to allow society to choose between the political programs of the present authorities and the opposition. A poll in the spring of 2001 found that most Russians believed that even the propresidential parties should criticize the policies of the top leadership when appropriate rather than automatically support the leadership's policies.[10]

First Priority Is to "Restore Order," but Order Is Not Authoritarianism

Opinion surveys indicate that most Russians are more worried at the current moment about restoring the state's ability to function effec-

Table 2-5. *Important Political Tasks*[a]
Percent

Tasks	Respondents
Development of national economic production	69
Preservation of Russia's status as a great power	35
Development of relations with other countries	24
Development and strengthening of democratic institutions and freedom of the press	12
Strengthening of the power vertical [that is, the central government's authority over regional and local units]	9

Source: Vtsiom public opinion survey, www.polit.ru, April 27, 2001.

a. "Choose from the following political tasks 4 to 5 which in your view best correspond to your interests and the interests of your family."

tively—to provide essential services—than about deepening democracy (see table 2-5). This focus is reflected in polling from the past decade that shows the population's first priority to be reviving economic growth and restoring the social safety net that diminished or disappeared in the 1990s. In one May 2000 poll that asked respondents to identify the government's main responsibilities, slightly more Russians chose "support for order in society" than chose "observation of human rights."[11]

This pattern of priorities is reflected in consistent support among the Russian public for a "strong hand" to deal with Russia's problems. Polls suggest that most Russians, while supporting the idea of a diffusion of power among branches of government, are more worried that the top leader will be too weak to tackle Russia's challenges than that he will gain so much power that he could undermine democratic freedoms. Polls in May 2000, for instance, showed majorities saying that Russia needed a concentration of power in a "single hand" and that, if President Putin were to establish "full control" over parliament and governors, it would be to Russia's benefit rather than detriment.

These findings reflect an understandable reaction to the impact on many Russian lives of the economic and social decline that began under communism and only accelerated in the first years of independent Russia. Placing a priority on order for most Russian citizens signifies support for actions that advance the state's capacity to provide physical security, create the rule of law, and pay salaries and pensions on time. There is nothing in the data to suggest widespread support for antidemocratic actions, that is, actions that would constrain individual liberties or restrict the right of Russian citizens to elect their leaders through open and honest elections.

Survey data exploring the political attitudes of those citizens who voted for Vladimir Putin for president in March 2000 support this understanding of the average Russian voter's priorities. Most of the citizens who voted for Putin, putting him over the top in the first round without the need for a runoff, expressed support for democratic values and institutions in an opinion survey conducted at the same time. Other polls indicate that, while large majorities of the public support strong leadership, they do not equate strong leadership with a subordination of civil liberties to the interests of the state.[12] Opinion surveys indicate that the proportion of Russian citizens supporting the notion that the interests of the state should take priority over their individual interests or those of their family has declined during the first post-Soviet decade (table 2-6).

Deep-Rooted Support for Democratic Values

The public opinion surveys discussed in this chapter, conducted by several Russian firms and prominent American scholars, are in general agreement about the pattern of public opinion since the end of the Soviet era. Some of the data suggest a modest ebbing of support for democratic values throughout the decade. Other data suggest little change or even a strengthening of support for democratic values. Overall, the clear impression is one of relative stability in public sentiment despite the economic hardships and political turmoil of the past decade. This stability suggests that popular attitudes about democracy are based on relatively durable calculations about the kind of society Russian citizens want to live in, attitudes formed over years and decades, rather than on a narrow calculation of immediate economic benefit.[13]

Table 2-6. *Changing Public Attitudes toward the State*
Percent

Attitude	1989 response	1999 response
Our state has given us everything: no one has a right to demand more	5	1
The state has provided us a lot, but it is possible to demand more	10	6
The state has given us so little that we are in no way obligated to it	7	38
Our state is now in such a situation that we should give it aid, even to the point of sacrifices	38	17
We should become free people and force the state to serve our interests	27	37
Other	1	2

Source: Yuriy Levada, "'Soviet Man' Ten Years Later: 1989–1999," published at www.polit.ru, January 17, 2001.

The failure of extremist political organizations from the right or the left to gain a significant foothold in post-Soviet Russia despite the seemingly propitious conditions is one more measure of how democratic values in Russia have become deeply rooted. Highly vocal groups supporting an antidemocratic agenda emerged along with those that came together under the umbrella of prodemocracy organizations as former leader Mikhail Gorbachev relaxed controls in the late 1980s, but according to historians of the period they never gained a significant following.[14]

Many Russian and Western political analysts in the early 1990s predicted that extremist parties who supported elements of a fascist or nationalist ideology would emerge as a significant threat unless market reforms quickly improved the lives of ordinary Russian citizens. The misnamed Liberal Democratic Party of Vladimir Zhirinovskiy (LDP), whose leaders espouse an eclectic mix of sometimes authoritarian and antidemocratic positions, received 23 percent of the vote in 1993, more than the largest prodemocracy party supported by President Yeltsin. Some studies suggest that a sizable portion of this total was from voters hoping to send a message of protest about former president Yeltsin's policies but not committed to authoritarian values. The LDP's support, in any event, declined sharply to 11 percent in the 1995 election and then again to 6 percent in the 1999 elections despite the deterioration in the living standards of most Russians throughout the decade. Recent polling suggests that the LDP's popularity remains at about the level it was in 1999.

The Russian Communist Party, many of whose members show a willingness to support antidemocratic positions, retained a sizable constituency throughout the 1990s, but the party has not been able to expand its support base despite the hardships brought on by market reforms. Many other extremist groups supporting fascist-like ideas have surfaced in post-Soviet Russia, but none of them has gained traction in the post-Soviet landscape despite the severe economic hardship facing ordinary Russian citizens.[15]

Historical Perspective on the Evolution of Russian Attitudes

Russian attitudes about democracy are based not on expedient factors such as the state of the economy but on fundamental changes in Russian society that have developed only gradually over decades and generations. No reliable public opinion survey data are available before the last years of the Soviet era. But historical studies support the notion that the breadth and depth of support in Russian society and the elite for a democratic political order have slowly but steadily expanded.

THE TSARIST ERA. The social base for democracy in the years leading up to the Russian Revolution encompassed only a thin slice of Russia's elite. Proponents of civil liberties and democratic values were pressured by supporters of more authoritarian methods on both sides— on the right by sizable segments of the elite who supported the monarchy and on the left by large and steadily growing numbers who supported radical social revolution. The autocracy's unwillingness to compromise contributed to a polarization of views and to the strength of radical elements on both sides of the political spectrum.

The political history of the last decades of the tsarist era suggests that support for democratic habits of political discourse—namely, tolerance of opposition and an ability to compromise—was also in short supply in the Russian elites. Neither the regime nor the majority of the democrati-cally minded elites in emerging political parties were willing to seek compromise at critical junctures, nourishing the political influence of the antidemocratic left.

Support for the democratic idea was even weaker outside the elite. The country was still overwhelmingly agricultural. Debate about polit-ical reform was largely the province of the elite. The demands of the rural population were focused on a redistribution of land. Most studies of popular sentiment in the countryside suggest a population unsym-pathetic with demands for democratic government and suspicious that democratic politicians in Russia's cities opposed a redistribution of land.[16]

THE SOVIET ERA. The limited data available to us about societal atti-tudes during the Soviet era suggest that support for democratic values and a liberalization of the state's authoritarian controls gradually deepened, especially in the years after Josef Stalin's death in 1953. The only system-atic studies of public opinion in this era—based on interviews of émigrés from the Soviet Union from the 1950s into the 1970s—suggest a growing demand for political liberalization dating to the early postwar years, with successive generations growing significantly more critical of the state's political controls.[17]

The spectrum of political opinion that emerged after most restraints on expression were removed in the late 1980s would seem to confirm that support for a more pluralistic political structure was widespread among the Russian people by the end of the Soviet era. The informal opposition organizations that emerged to oppose the Communist Party elite's monopoly on political power included a wide range of views on many issues, but there was near unanimity on abolishing the Communist Party's monopoly and replacing it with a more pluralistic arrangement. Gradually growing support for democratic values is consistent also with polling data that show larger numbers of Russians identifying them-selves as European (figure 2-3).

Studies of democratic patterns globally suggest a strong correlation between economic development and education and the support for

Figure 2-3. *Russian Identity*[a]

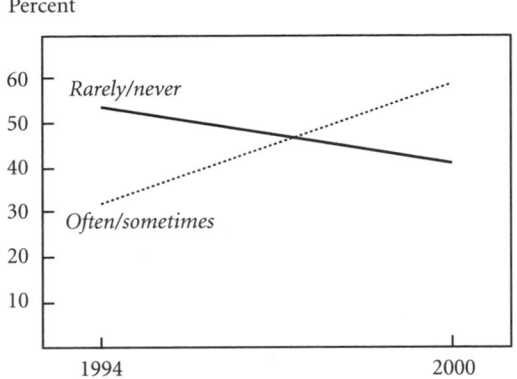

Percent

Source: Rose and Haerpfer, *New Russia Barometer III*, p. 43; Richard Rose, *Russia Elects a President: New Russia Barometer IX*, Studies in Public Policy 330 (University of Strathclyde, Centre for the Study of Public Policy, 2000), p. 42.
a. In 1994: "Do you ever think of yourself not only as a citizen of Russia but also as a European?" In 2000: "Do you ever think of yourself as a European?"

democratic forms of governance. It is plausible that the dramatic increases in education levels, urbanization, and economic development under the Soviet regime provided the social basis for greater support for civil liberties and democratic values. Although it can not be proved, it is also plausible that the Soviet regime's decision to adopt the rhetoric of democracy in formal documents and public statements nourished the growth of the idea that democracy was the only legitimate political order and encouraged cynicism about the gap between the rhetoric and the reality of Soviet institutions, which ultimately helped to undermine popular support for the USSR.

Desire to Build Democracy in a Russian Way

Responses to opinion surveys send a clear message that Russians do not want Western states to tell them how to build democracy in Russia and that Russians have a new appreciation for the difficulty of transplanting foreign models of economic and political institutions onto Russian soil. Polls that offer Russian citizens a choice between a political system such

Figure 2-4. *Opinion on Political System, 1994 and 1999*[a]

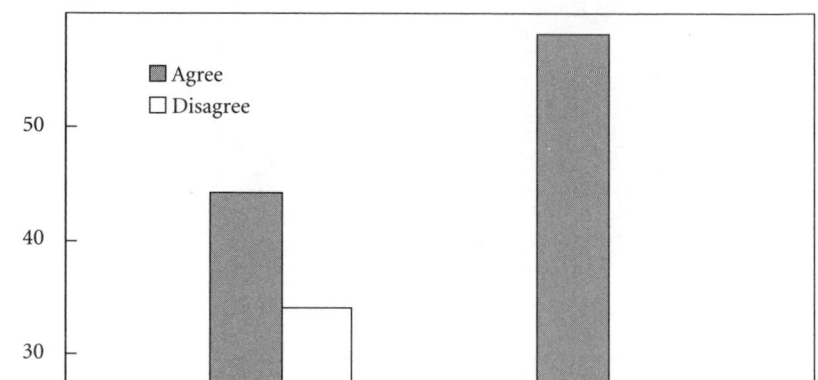

Source: Levada, "'Soviet Man' Ten Years Later."
a. "It would have been better if everything in the country had remained as before 1985." Figure does not include "hard to say" responses.

as that of the former Soviet Union and a democracy "of the Western type" invariably show that a plurality of Russians favor the Soviet-type system (figure 2-4). In a similar manner, surveys that offer Russians a choice between their own, unique path in building a political system and a democratic path of the "Western type" show Russians favoring their own path. The proportion of Russians endorsing something different from "democracy of the Western type" has grown during the past decade along with economic hardship and the failure of Russian leaders to deal with entrenched official corruption.

Other polling data allow us to interpret the meaning of this widespread sentiment in Russia today. These data indicate that this pattern of

Figure 2-5. *Preferred Political System for Russia, 1999–2000*[a]

Percent

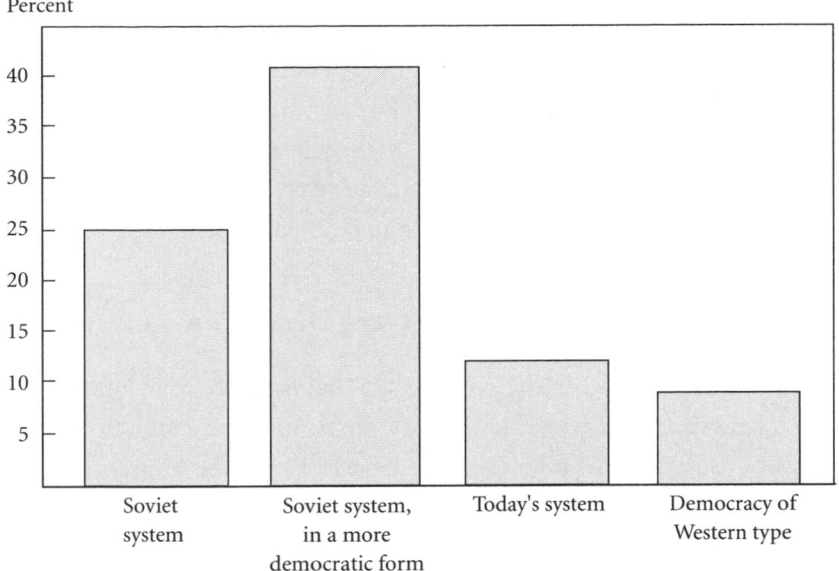

Source: Colton and McFaul, "Are Russians Undemocratic?" p. 7.
a. Figure does not include "don't know" responses.

response has nothing to do with support for the authoritarian attributes of the Soviet political system and everything to do with popular support for state-supported social and economic protections for the population often associated with the Soviet era, protections that post-Soviet institutions were unable to sustain. When they are offered a different choice—between a Soviet-type system and a Soviet-type system but in a different, more democratic form, more Russians choose the latter than the former (figure 2-5). Similarly, other polls show that, when given the choice of continuing the reforms of the 1990s but with social protections for the population, more members of the public choose that option than choose "returning to socialism."

Surveys of Russian opinion indicate that a homegrown democracy in Russia is likely to feature a more paternalistic state than most American proponents of democracy would favor. Russian democracy could feature a considerable role for the state in providing social guarantees to the

Russian population and mitigating the potential inegalitarian extremes of a market economy. Studies of Soviet émigré opinion, popular opinion from the last days of the Soviet Union under Mikhail Gorbachev, and data from recent years show that large numbers of Russians consistently show support for a strong state role in providing social and economic guarantees. These studies show consistently lower support for reforms designed to reduce the role of the state in the economy than for reforms designed to reduce the state's role in the political system.[18]

Support for Leaders Who Build Strong Democratic Institutions

There is no ambiguity in the polling data that measure how Russian citizens believe their formal democratic institutions are functioning in practice. Russians' confidence in their parliament (the Supreme Soviet until 1993 and thereafter the Federal Assembly) dropped steadily in the early and mid-1990s until reaching a very low level, where it has stayed since that time (figure 2-6). Russians offer largely negative responses to questions that ask whether voting gives them some say in how their government is run. Large majorities express little or no confidence in the court system. Russians' deep skepticism about their political institutions is underscored by the results of opinion surveys that compare attitudes of Russian citizens about their current institutions to those of publics in other countries. These surveys show Russians as more negative about their institutions than the vast majority of other publics polled.[19]

Those who study the history of democracy underscore the critical role that competition among various political parties plays in creating a stable, healthy democratic system. Russians express very low confidence in political parties (figure 2-7). Surveys that explore the kind of party system Russians would prefer show that the political turmoil of the 1990s brought disillusionment with the benefits of multiparty politics. In the early 1990s relatively solid majorities agreed that Russia needed a multiparty system. By 1999, however, results were more mixed (table 2-7).[20]

Figure 2-6. *Confidence in Parliament*[a]

Percent expressing "little or no confidence"

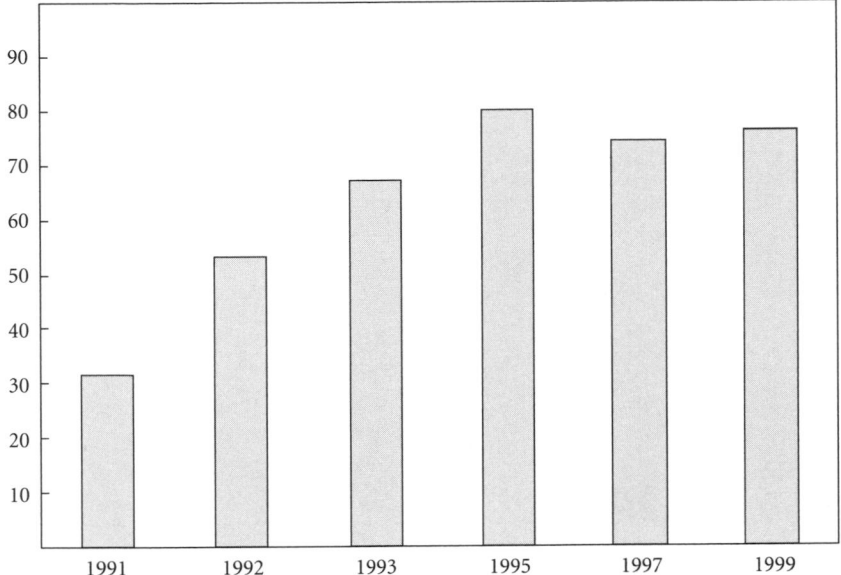

Source: USIA, "How Unsteady Is Russian Democracy?"; Dobson, "Is Russia Turning the Corner?";
USIA, Office of Research and Media Reaction, "Russians Value Civil Liberties, but Know They Are a
Long Way from Democracy, Rule of Law," Opinion Analysis M-158-99 (August 6, 1999).

a. "Please tell me how much confidence you have in each of the following institutions—Parliament."

The disdain that overwhelming majorities of Russians exhibit about
their current political institutions suggests that most Russians understand the meaning of the democratic values they claim to support and
are convinced that their current institutions do not do a good job of
providing those values. The majorities who support democratic values
while expressing disdain for current institutions suggests a willingness,
if not to demand more democratic institutions, at least to support political leaders who seek to make Russia's current institutions more
democratic and effective.

Polling data suggest that actions by their leaders to create a stronger
judiciary and an impartial court system are a high priority for Russian

Figure 2-7. *Trust in Russian Political Parties*[a]

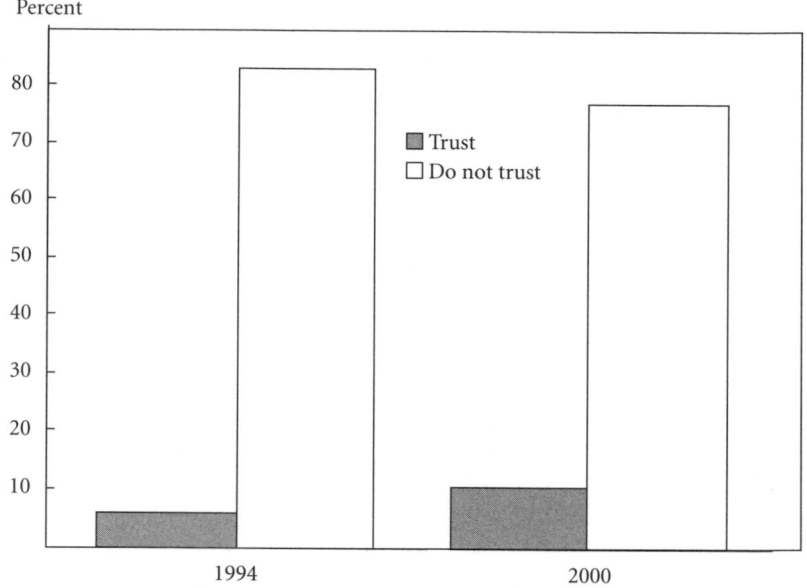

Percent

Source: Rose and Haerpfer, *New Russia Barometer III*, p. 31; and Rose, *Russia Elects a President*, p. 28.
a. "To what extent do you trust each of the following institutions to look after your interests—Political parties?" Figure does not include "neutral" responses.

citizens. Surveys from as early as 1993 show that, when they were asked to select the most important attributes of a "democratic" society, Russians placed a "judicial system that treats everyone fairly" at the top of their list, well above a "free market economy." Similarly, when they were asked to choose from a menu of the most important attributes of the society they would like to live in, Russians in 1997 put "a judicial system that treats everyone fairly and punishes the guilty whoever they are" at the top of the list.[21]

Resistance Centered in a Small Segment of Political and Economic Elite

The political attitudes of Russia's elites are arguably more important than the attitudes of the general public in a society in which political par-

Table 2-7. *Attitude toward a Multiparty System,*
by Education of Respondents[a]
Percent

Educational level	One-party system	Two-party system	Multiparty system
All respondents	48	52[b]	52[b]
Less than secondary education	69	8	31
Secondary education	43	12	45
Higher education	19	16	65

Source: USIA, Office of Research and Media Reaction, "Russians Favor Moscow Mayor's Party, Communists," Opinion Analysis M-160-99 (August 12, 1999).
a. "Would you prefer a one-party, two-party, or multiparty system?"
b. 52 percent support either a two-party or a multiparty system.

ties and citizen activism remain weak. Liberalizing reforms in Russia, including those under Gorbachev and Yeltsin, have historically been initiated (though not always controlled) by its political elite.

Some analysts of Russian affairs argue that there is less support for democratic values among the Russian elite than among the mass public.[22] This argument is often linked with the conviction that reviving Russia's status as a great power is more important to the elite than to the public at large, and that many in the elite believe that authoritarian measures may be needed to accomplish this goal.

Systematic efforts to measure elite opinion do not support the assertion that antidemocratic attitudes are more widespread in the Russian elite as a whole than among the mass public. On the contrary, the data show that elites by substantial margins are more strongly committed to democratic values (and even more so to a market economy) than the public at large. Survey data from polls that measure the sentiment of various segments of the elite in the early and mid-1990s consistently showed greater support for democratic values than among the public.[23] A recently published review of survey data from 1993 to 1999 suggests that this pattern has held steady through the period (figure 2-8).

Other polling data reinforce the impession of stronger support for democratic values among Russian elites than among the public, some-

Figure 2-8. *Elite and Mass Public Support for Democratic Values*[a]

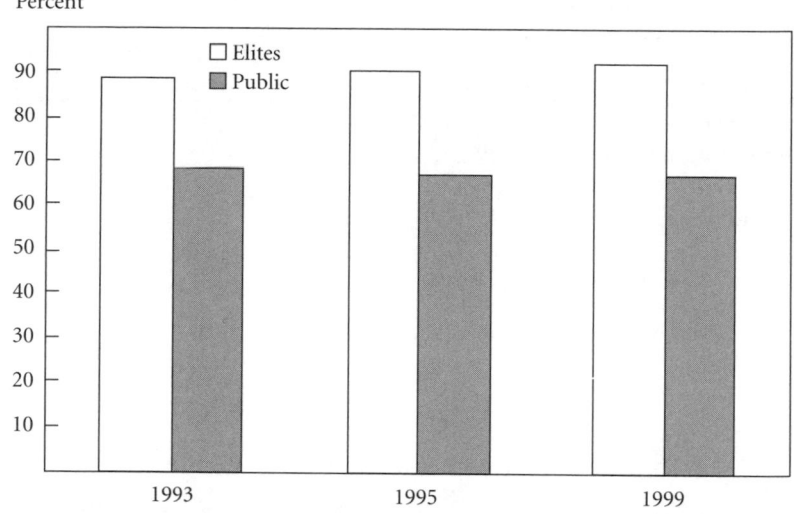

Percent

Source: Author's calculations based on data derived from William Zimmerman, *The Russian People and Foreign Policy: Elite and Mass Perspectives 1993–2000* (Princeton University Press, 2002), pp. 14–18 and table 3, p. 56.

a. Zimmerman pulls together several surveys from these three years and divides elites and the public into liberal democrats, social democrats, market authoritarians, and socialist authoritarians, based on aggregating the results of several separate survey questions. I have aggregated the two varieties of democrat and the two varieties of authoritarian. Zimmerman's data show many more social democrats—that is, those who support a strong state role in the economy—among the public than among the elite.

times by sizable margins. Polls indicate, for instance, that there is far less support among the elite than among the public for the idea that at times a concentration of power in a single hand is needed or that violating human rights is acceptable if necessary to restore order. A greater proportion of Russia's elites also express appreciation for the potential benefits of competition among political parties.[24]

That elites show stronger support for democratic values than the mass public should not be a surprise. It is a common pattern across the globe. This pattern is consistent with public opinion survey results that show noticeably higher support for democratic values among individuals with a higher education and a higher income than among the population as a whole. Members of the elite typically have higher levels of education and income than the general public.

These data on Russia's elite attitudes, as well as studies of the nature of post-Soviet Russian politics as it emerged under former president Yeltsin, suggest that resistance to steps toward deeper democracy is centered not in the elite as a whole but in a tiny minority of the Russian elite that benefits from economic advantage and privileged access to political power in the current system and is therefore opposed to changes in the status quo. A fortunate few, many of them already in positions of influence in the last years of the Soviet era, were able to take advantage of the collapse of Soviet power and the rapid and relatively unregulated push toward privatization of state property to gain substantial economic wealth in a short period. The economic wealth and privilege of many of them depend on insider advantages they were able to obtain, and continue to obtain, from corrupt relationships with government officials, which yield government policies and regulations to their benefit. The lack of strong political institutions, and the inability of the Russian government to implement even those well-intended policies adopted in the 1990s, created a political environment in which these corrupt relationships could flourish.[25]

Failures Blamed on Poor Leadership, Not on Democracy

Many Western accounts link the shortcomings of Russia's new democracy to weak support for democracy in Russian society and the lack of a democratic political culture. But Russians identify more proximate causes. They link the difficulties of the past decade to the policies of those Russian leaders who launched Russia's experiment with democratic and market economy reforms. In one 1999 survey, "weak and incompetent leaders" was the response most often volunteered by Russian citizens when they were asked to identify the causes for the failure of the country to make a successful transition to democracy. "Ineffective political leadership" was also the response most often offered when Russians were invited to identify the most important political failure during these years.[26]

Polling data indicate that far more Russians blame Yeltsin and Gorbachev for the difficulties Russia now faces than blame Soviet leaders who preceded the Gorbachev leadership's decision to institute liberalizing reforms. When they were asked in December 2000 if the Yeltsin era brought more harm or more good for Russia, Russian citizens chose harm by 75 to 15 percent.[27]

Political historians will have to credit Yeltsin with success in accomplishing what he considered his most important task—setting Russia on the road to a more open society and ensuring the thorough destruction of the old, communist order. But many Russian and Western historians agree that Yeltsin—Russia's president from 1990 until the end of the decade—and his governments can be assigned significant blame for Russia's failure to build stronger and more effective democratic institutions. They fault Yeltsin for not moving more quickly after the collapse of the Soviet Union to consolidate support for a new democratic structure through a new constitution and a "founding election" that could have united most Russians behind a new political order before controversial and painful economic reforms were launched.[28] The reactionary and authoritarian cast of many Russian legislators—elected in the Soviet era under rules that favored retention of large numbers of the existing elite—provided fertile soil for opposition to Yeltsin's plans for rapid economic liberalization, once the social costs of that course began to register. The widespread support for Yeltsin personally and evidence of public support for radical steps to deal with the paralysis that characterized the last Gorbachev years provided a window for new presidential and legislative elections that could have put much of this elite out to pasture and solidified public support for new directions. Some prodemocratic forces pushed for early elections. They extracted a promise of early elections from Yeltsin in early 1992, but the elections never occurred.[29]

In this instance and in subsequent years, Yeltsin never made the development of new institutions and the implementation of structural reforms a priority. Although he was urged by some in the prodemocracy camp to associate himself directly with a political party, as a way to encourage party development, Yeltsin never did so. In retrospect, Russian analysts from both ends of the political spectrum who agree on little else agree that Yeltsin failed to use his personal authority to push for needed structural changes and institutional development.

Many students of Yeltsin's leadership have attributed this pattern of behavior to his preference for a personalized style of rule and reluctance to support the creation of institutions that he would not be able to control.[30] The lack of commitment to building strong democratic institutions opened the way for the development of a political system in post-Soviet Russia in which informal networks and privileged groups had inordinate influence on political and economic decisions. These insiders were able to profit from the move to a market economy at the expense of ordinary citizens. Rather than taking decisive action to create strong institutions capable of controlling and diluting the influence of such insiders, Yeltsin was content to serve as an umpire refereeing their often bitter disputes over power and property. Formal democratic institutions remained weak, and democratic habits had little opportunity to develop.

Many regional elites who benefited from Yeltsin's encouragement of regional autonomy and from the early stages of the privatization of the economy developed this same bias against the development of strong and effective political institutions.[31] Thus the way was opened up for the growth of popular cynicism about Russia's democratic institutions, and the road was blocked to the growth of greater societal consensus around democratic norms.

The way Yeltsin and other members of the ruling group made decisions, as well as the decisions they made, can be assigned part of the blame that the democratic idea did not take stronger root. Willingness to compromise, an essential political habit in a strong democratic system, was seen as a sign of weakness rather than strength in the Soviet political culture. The political history of the Yeltsin decade suggests that democratic habits of discourse—tolerance of opposition and willing-ness to compromise—were in short supply in Yeltsin's approach to leadership and in the approach taken by other members of the ruling elite. More difficult for Russia than accepting the values of democracy was the process of rejecting the binary understanding of political power—if you win, I lose—and accepting the benefits of compromise, humility, and incremental gains.[32] Yeltsin, in the end, chose force rather than compromise to deal with the deep divisions that developed in the early 1990s over the shape of the new political order that should replace the Soviet system, and he acted outside the constitution to disband the parliament in October 1993 and schedule new elections.

Leaders of Russia's most prodemocratic political parties (called "democrats" at the time and typically referred to as "liberals" today) take their share of the blame. Key liberal politicians were directly associated with Yeltsin's policy choices, including the decision to focus initially on market reform rather than political reform and an approach to market reform that worked to enrich a handful of insiders while impoverishing large segments of the population. Many historians also blame the splin-tering of the Russian liberals and their weak showing in the elections of the 1990s on their inability to compromise sufficiently to run on a com-mon platform. Liberal parties—still the most forceful proponents of movement toward deeper democracy in Russia today—typically draw the support of 15 to 20 percent of the population in opinion polls and leadership elections, far below the share of the population that professes support for democratic values.

As a whole, the available data about popular attitudes toward democ-racy and the historical record of elite politics in Russia in the 1990s suggest support for a thesis set out by James Gibson in 1996: that it is not so much the shortfall of democratic values in the public at large that should concern proponents of Russian democracy but "the degree to which political elites can agree to compete for political power through the ordinary (and orderly) mechanisms of democracy"[33] (box 2-2).

Box 2-2. *Russia's Political Spectrum*

Russia's political spectrum, along with its nomenclature, has evolved substantially since the initial flowering of open political opposition and official sanction for pluralism in the last years of the Soviet Union. In the late 1980s and early 1990s, those who were pressing the government for liberalization and democratic institutions described themselves as "democrats" and were commonly referred to as such by Russian and Western analysts. They were opposed by various political forces, including the Communist Party, who resisted democratic change and supported some variety of a more authoritarian or state-centered political order.

Since the mid-1990s, Russians have increasingly described their political reality along a spectrum from "right" to "left" and have ordered their political universe by placing political parties and groups along this spectrum. In this emerging political nomenclature, the right side of the political spectrum is occupied by parties and organizations that describe themselves as liberals. Liberals in the classical European sense of the term, they seek to shrink the traditionally intrusive role of the state and government institutions and expand the realm of private activity and protections for individual liberties. Most liberal politicians support the thrust of the Putin government's liberalizing economic program while opposing policies that increase the state's authorities to regulate and control independent political and societal institutions.

Communists, who generally support the president's state-centered policies on the political front but oppose his economic program, anchor the left side of the spectrum. Continuing skepticism among the Russian public about the communists on the left and disillusionment with the liberals on the right have opened the way to a dominant role for a variety of centrist parties whose only coherent ideology is support for the president. The ill-named Liberal Democratic Party (LDP) of Vladimir Zhirinovskiy does not fit easily into this nomenclature. The LDP often supports authoritarian positions on the political front but liberal positions on the economic front.

As one measure of their relative clout, liberal parties currently hold about 50 seats in the 450-seat State Duma, while pro-Communist deputies hold around 130.

Russia's Leaders and the Unfinished Democratic Agenda

The data presented underscore the Russian leadership's unfinished democratic agenda. The Soviet legacy and the turmoil of the Yeltsin years have left Russian society divided. Though majorities consistently support democratic values, the numbers who say they do not, or who do not see building stronger democratic institutions as a policy priority, remain sizable. Many of the survey questions show large gaps in attitudes about democracy between older and younger citizens, individuals with higher education and those without, urban dwellers and citizens of the country, and citizens with relatively high and low incomes. The hardship of the 1990s did not produce a significant shift away from support for democratic values, but it prevented a consolidation of support in society for a democratic path.

The data presented also indicate that the responsibility for this unfinished agenda lies not with Russian society and not even with the Russian elite, but with the relatively narrow segment of the elite that benefits from limits on democracy and is threatened by action to construct more vibrant democratic institutions.

No one should expect Russian society to organize itself to demand deeper democracy. Decades of suppression by Soviet authorities of independent political groups and years of indifference by the post-Soviet leadership toward the task of building strong political institutions have left most Russians cynical about government and skeptical that organizing to press demands on the state will be worth the effort.[34] There is nothing in the data about political attitudes that suggests Russians are prepared to go into the streets to fight for democratic change. Data from the World Values Survey indicate that Russians rank relatively low on measures such as "self-expression" or interpersonal trust that are typically correlated with the kind of citizen activism that provides impetus to stronger institutions in most established democracies.[35]

Understandably, most Russians are focused on the struggle to provide a better life for themselves and their families. Their top priority is a

Russian state strong and effective enough to create the conditions for a just society and sustained economic growth. Russia's leaders and political elites, not the average citizen, must show the political will to create the strong democratic institutions that will encourage the growth of civil society and citizen activism and provide the most reliable route to a strong and effective state.

3

Shifting toward Faster Democratic Development

When a political system is mired in stagnation . . . the winning political strategy is to propagate an "idea whose time has come."

U.S. political scientist George Breslauer[1]

The anticommunist, pro-Western atmosphere that dominated Moscow in the immediate wake of the collapse of the Soviet Union provided a propitious climate for those in the leadership who hoped to move Russia quickly toward Western-style democratic institutions. Through legislation and presidential decree, Russia put in place much of the legal framework necessary to support a robust democratic order, including a new, more democratic constitution, a new parliament patterned on European models, and new laws protecting freedom of the press and enhancing the independence of the judicial branch.

The political climate began shifting against proponents of further movement toward Western-style democratic institutions early in Boris Yeltsin's tenure. This shift was prompted by a reaction to the political instability seemingly produced by Russia's new democratic institutions—symbolized in the violence between supporters of President Yeltsin and his reforms and the opposition-led parliament in October 1993—and the economic hardship that many Russians linked to the removal of price controls, privatization, and other moves toward the market. While dedicated to preventing the communists from returning to power and to protecting a pluralistic system, Yeltsin quickly tacked toward his opponents and brought conservative officials into his administration. Their commitment to Western-style institutions and a free market economy was suspect. The kind of structural reforms needed to create a durable basis for a market economy and a vigorous democracy made little progress during the rest of the Yeltsin era.

By the end of the 1990s, the main issue in Russia's political elite became not how to expand democracy but how to halt the deterioration of the capacity of the Russian state and the demographic and economic decline that accompanied the failure of the leadership to make a decisive breakthrough toward new institutions.

The failure of Russia's first democratic leaders to create political stability, economic justice, or economic growth has led to new respectability in the elite for those who advocate a more authoritarian approach to the task of creating Russia's new political and economic institutions. These critics favor a strong guiding role by the government in Russia's political development to maintain political stability and ensure that the articulation of various points of view remains within bounds consistent with what the government believes is compatible with rebuilding a strong state. They believe that authoritarian methods are needed to repair the anarchy and decline they attribute to the Yeltsin era and to restore Russia's stature as a strong state and a great power. Many of them are particularly aggrieved by the decline in the central government's authority in Russia under Yeltsin and the degree to which Russia's regional governors and owners of Russia's largest business conglomerates exploited the state's weakness to augment their power and privileges. Some political observers in Russia and the West have described the goal of the proponents of these policies as "controlled" or "managed" democracy.[2]

Some of the proponents of managed democracy make the case that Russia's history of top-down reform and the relative weakness of nongovernment organizations justify a prominent role for the state in organizing and leading Russia's political development. Some Russian analysts have also offered support to the idea of managed democracy by arguing that a temporary period of benign dictatorship is acceptable or even needed to prevent developments that could lead to a more severe form of authoritarianism.

This shift in opinion is not about the philosophical issue of whether democracy is the right political order for Russia. There is no serious discussion about alternatives to democracy. Many proponents of policies associated with managed democracy would insist that their policies are designed to encourage democracy's growth in Russian conditions. Their point of view is often apparent publicly in suggestions that Russia will at the right time need to take additional steps to adopt Western-style democratic institutions—such as a government formed on the basis of a majority coalition in parliament—but that the time is not yet ripe for such steps.

President Putin's Approach to Democracy

The policies of the Putin administration so far have reflected the dominant position that the ideas associated with managed democracy had assumed in Russia's political elite by the time President Putin took power in January 2000 following Yeltsin's premature resignation. His first actions in office underscored the priority he placed on reducing the oversized political role that regional governors and the leaders of Russia's largest business conglomerates had come to play in the last years of the Yeltsin era and on gathering back into the Kremlin some of the power that had flowed out to the governors and oligarchs. For example,

—To facilitate a deal with Russia's governors to terminate their ex officio status as members of the parliament's upper house, Putin acceded to new legislation that made democratically elected mayors of Russia's cities subject to dismissal by the governors. The governors were replaced with appointed representatives from the regions.

Box 3-1. *The Decline of the Eurasianists*

Some political forces in Russia continue to raise the idea that Russia should seek to find its own "third way" separate from that of the communist era but also separate from that of the West. Many of the adherents of this point of view are taking aim not at democracy but at the process of globalization that they associate with Western-style institutions and at globalization's potentially significant impact on Russia. They support ill-defined measures that would somehow allow Russia to prosper without full integration with global economic and political institutions. Some proponents of this point of view attempt to give it an ideological basis by arguing that Russian civilization took a separate and superior course to Western civilization early in its history, that it is by history and culture a "Eurasian" rather than a European power, and that these fundamental differences are enduring. They compare Russia's more collectivist culture to what they see as excessive individualism and materialism in the West. They argue that Russia should seek to encourage a Eurasian community with its neighbors as an alternative to integration with global institutions.[1]

—In taking action to limit the political role of the owners of Russia's largest business conglomerates, Putin condoned actions by government agencies that have increased state control of national media by transferring controlling ownership of several major media companies from the oligarchs to government-connected entities or to private owners more sympathetic to the administration's point of view.

The focus on controlling rather than encouraging independent initiative in the political arena is underscored by the strikingly different philosophy that has appeared to motivate the Putin administration's actions in the economic arena. His support for policies that shrink the role of the state in the economy and encourage private initiative has been apparent both in rhetoric—notably his State of the Federation addresses to Russia's parliament in March 2001 and April 2002—and in actions. The administration has introduced and pushed through the leg-

These points of view find some support in intellectual circles, among nationalist elements on the left side of the political spectrum, in the Russian Orthodox church, and in business circles that would stand to lose from globalization. Organizations encouraging Russia to follow a course separate from the West were encouraged by Putin's focus in some of his early public remarks on the strong, paternalistic role that the state has played in Russian history. But they are influential largely on the fringes of the political spectrum.

1. A good overview of the sentiments of those who call for Russia to follow a distinct path separate from Western civilization can be found in Yuri Fedorov, "Democratization and Globalization: The Case of Russia," Working Paper 13 (Washington: Carnegie Endowment for International Peace, May 2000), pp. 12–24. Recent assessments of the program and prospects of political groups that call for Russia to follow a separate "Eurasian" course include Victor Yasmann, "The Rise of the Eurasians," *RFE/RL Security Watch*, vol. 12, no. 17 (April 30, 2001); Aleksandr Maksimov and Orkhan Karabaagi, "The Eurasians Have Been Recruited to Serve the Sovereign," *Obshchaya Gazeta*, May 31, 2001; Zbigniew Brzezinski, "A Plan for Europe," *Foreign Affairs*, vol. 74 (January–February 1995), p. 31, discusses this debate between "Eurasianists" and "Europeanists" in the mid-1990s.

islature strongly promarket structural reforms, such as a reduction in income tax rates and measures to shrink the government's regulatory role in the economy.

The Putin administration's guiding philosophy in its first years is well illustrated in its early initiatives on policies affecting freedom of expression and development of Russia's still weakly developed political party system. On both fronts, the administration's initiatives convey an intent to restore momentum to the process of building stronger political and economic institutions that flagged under Yeltsin and at the same time to retain for the state the right to control how those institutions operate and the ability to limit political opposition.[3]

—A key document governing policy on media and political expression, the "Information Security Doctrine" signed by the president and published in September 2000, contains provisions that could work to encourage pluralism in the news media and improved access by Russian citizens to information sources. But it also contains language that could justify a stepped-up effort by state institutions to control the flow of information. It explicitly cites the need to balance the interests of the individual against the interests of the state, and it conveys an expanded definition of national security that could justify state intervention to regulate freedom of expression.[4]

—Some provisions of a new law adopted in 2001 governing the activity of Russia's political parties—such as minimum membership requirements in half of Russia's eighty-nine regions—along with separate legislation backed by the administration in 2002 that mandates proportional representation and party list voting in regional legislatures—could stimulate parties to put down deeper roots in Russia's regions and increase their role in politics. But the law also contains provisions—such as registration requirements and state financing—that would give the state new levers to regulate and control parties and restrict the activities of those that it finds distasteful.[5]

The same set of dual objectives appears to have motivated the Putin administration's policies toward the public role of the nongovernment organizations, professional groups, and advocacy organizations that make up Russia's "civil society."

—The Putin administration has given new visibility to nongovernment organizations, and in a meeting with NGO leaders in 2001 Putin indicated the intention of the administration to establish regular contacts between the state and leading nongovernment groups. Increased visibility for civil society institutions could give impetus to their membership and activity. But the administration can also use government involvement as one more tool to manage Russia's political scene, favoring those organizations it prefers over others that may be too vociferous in challenging the administration and the government.[6]

The spirit of state control evident in the pattern of policies and pronouncements from the Putin administration has encouraged other Russian government agencies as well as leaders at the regional level to seek to impose a broad pattern of constraints on democratic development in Russia. These signals from the Kremlin have served to legitimize actions by state agencies to intimidate journalists and citizen activists who challenge government policies with excessive zeal and to condone actions by authorities at several levels to manipulate the results of elections.

Putin's rhetoric about democracy since he took office conveys the same duality as his administration's actions. He has been articulate and adamant in saying that building Western-style democratic institutions is Russia's only viable way forward. He has gone well beyond platitudes:

—He has said that Russia needs strong national political parties.

—He has emphasized the importance of a judiciary independent from the executive branch. He has repeatedly expressed support for freedom of the press, though usually in response to interviewers who question his support.

—He has insisted that political opposition goes along with democracy.

—He has called for a strong civil society to monitor political authorities, describing executive authority as the "main threat" to individual rights.

Even before his tilt toward support for the United States following September 11, Putin explicitly rejected the idea that there is any point in seeking a "third way" that attempts to somehow balance between East and West. He has distanced himself from those who oppose a rapid entry into global institutions and said Russia must take the same path that Europe has taken.

At the same time, Putin's public remarks convey caution and concern about actions that would move Russia more resolutely toward Western-style democratic institutions in the near term. He has asserted that Russian history has produced a political climate in which Russia cannot simply adopt European institutions wholesale. He has said that the Russian people expect the state to play a strong role. And he has on several occasions suggested that Russia was simply not yet ready for certain steps, such as a government formed on the basis of a parliamentary majority, or

Box 3-2. *The Russian Political System*

The 1993 constitution, which set the basic parameters of the Russian political system, was shaped by former president Yeltsin's determination to restrict the ability of his political opponents in the legislature to interfere with his vision for the new Russian state. As a result it creates what many have called a "superpresidency."

The constitution provides for a formal separation of powers. The president can issue decrees, veto legislation passed by the parliament—the Federal Assembly—and dissolve the parliament and call new elections under certain conditions. The Federal Assembly can in turn override presidential vetoes and initiate impeachment of the president. The supreme court of the land, the Constitutional Court, can invalidate on constitutional grounds legislation passed by the Federal Assembly and decrees issued by the president.

As the history of Russia's first decade shows, these constitutional provisions have created real checks on the ability of the president to act unilaterally. But a number of constitutional provisions—and a tradition of strong executive power in Russia—tilt the locus of power in this arrangement toward the president:

—The president has expansive decree powers;

—The government is selected by the president and not on the basis of the parliamentary majority;

the president joining a political party, that could accelerate development of democratic institutions.[7]

The president's comments about freedom of expression have shown passion only when he has attacked what he describes as abuses of press freedom by some of Russia's "oligarchs." He has passed up numerous opportunities to put himself on record as a partisan advocate of freedom of expression and a critic of actions by government or nongovernment actors that have the effect of diminishing the ability of political opponents to state their case.

—Parliamentary approval of presidential appointees is required only for the prime minister, the attorney general, and the chair of the central bank;

—Parliament's power to oversee and investigate the executive branch is highly restricted; and

—Impeachment is a highly cumbersome process involving action by the supreme and constitutional courts as well as both houses of parliament.

The president is elected by popular vote for a four-year term and can serve no more than two terms.

The Federal Assembly's upper house, the Federation Council, consists of two representatives from each of the country's eighty-nine regions. These representatives are appointed by each region's leadership. The lower house, the State Duma, is made up of 450 representatives elected for four-year terms. Two hundred and twenty-five deputies are elected by nationwide party list ballot, while the other 225 are elected in single-member districts.

In any country the formal structures do not reflect the degree to which well-connected elites and other insiders influence decisions through informal networks. In Russia this problem is exacerbated because the country lacks the strong political parties that in vigorous democracies force much of the backroom politics into the light of day and serve to organize and channel public needs into the formal political system. It also lacks a strong network of politically active nongovernment organizations whose representations to elected leaders can counterbalance the influence of vested interests.

Friends and Foes of Managed Democracy in the Elite

It is impossible to precisely define the locus or the extent of support for the policies associated with managed democracy inside Russia's political establishment. Even the proponents of managed democracy adopt democracy's rhetoric in public discourse, and few are willing to be caught openly favoring controls on political expression. Some of its most committed advocates can be found in the senior levels of Russia's federal bureaucracy, especially among the national security and intelligence agencies and in President Putin's own administration. President Putin has relied heavily on senior officials from the intelligence agencies to staff his administration.

Many of these officials, who operate largely outside the public political arena, seem convinced that rebuilding the power of the central government and the Russian state should be Russia's first priority and that the political turmoil and economic decline inherited from the Yeltsin era justify at least a "soft" form of authoritarianism in pursuit of that objective. Political elites in many of Russia's eighty-nine regional governments and individual business leaders who benefit from insider advantages in the current arrangement are also likely to oppose more aggressive efforts to build a deeper democracy.[8]

Many of the proponents of managed democracy are also among the most ardent skeptics of deeper cooperation with the United States and the policies of closer alignment with the United States and the West that President Putin approved after September 11. They are deeply skeptical about U.S. intentions, believing that the United States seeks to exploit and perpetuate Russia's weakness. As a result they see Russia's path toward renewal as not so much in integration as in competition with the West, and they tend to see relations with Western powers as a zero-sum game.

In Russia's public political arena, policies associated with managed democracy have received their most reliable support from political parties in the parliament that dominate the middle of the Russian political spectrum. Many political figures from these parties were elected on Putin's coattails in the 1999 legislative elections, and they see their future as tied to an ability to win additional favors from the Putin administration. Their support for the policies of managed democracy is not based on ideology as much as on political calculation. As such, they are comfortable combining support for the administration's free market economic policies with equally enthusiastic support for antidemocratic initiatives. Leaders of the Unity Party, formed with Putin's encouragement in advance of the 1999 parliamentary elections and since merged with other centrist parties to form United Russia, say they stand for "conservatism in politics and free development in economics."[9]

Data from surveys of Russia's legislators suggest that the pattern of repeated votes to support the Presidential Administration's legislative priorities on the political front disguises considerable diversity of political views in these centrist political parties and ambivalent attitudes at best about adding to the authorities of the state bureaucracy to regulate the country's political life. Many centrist politicians, for instance, out of a sense of self-preservation, have expressed reservations about the freedom that the new law governing political parties would give to the executive branch to regulate political parties and ban those that it finds objectionable.[10]

The policies of managed democracy have also drawn support from political figures associated with the Communist Party and other elements of the left side of Russia's political spectrum. Leaders on the left, many of whom lament the collapse of the Soviet system, have welcomed steps to rebuild and glorify the state and augment its authorities. Even the communists are not unified: some party officials have shown concern, in light of the history of former president Yeltsin's pitched battle against the party, that the new law on political parties could be used to control their activities or ban the party altogether. Communist Party leaders have openly opposed the Putin administration's market-oriented economic program and its turn toward closer cooperation with the United States after September 11. They have shifted toward open opposition to the government despite support for some of its state-centered policies on the political front.[11]

In the public political arena, the most forthright opposition to the policies of managed democracy has come from party leaders on the right or "liberal" wing of the Russian political spectrum, primarily centered around the political parties Yabloko and the Union of Right Forces. As set forth in the program documents of the two parties, they support policies that would accelerate Russia's adoption of Western-style institutions rather than treat them as a goal for which Russia is not yet ready.[12] The liberals have with some success sought to resist or water down Putin administration initiatives—such as elements of the law governing political parties—that would give the federal bureaucracies increased legislative sanction for intervening to regulate private political and economic activity.

Most Russian liberals support the Putin administration's free-market economic policies and in fact take credit for helping to shape them. Most support efforts to restore state capacity and enhance the authority of the federal government while placing constraints on the independence that regional authorities had accrued under Yeltsin. They accept the need for steps that encourage political stability in the wake of the turbulence of the Yeltsin years.

Russia's liberals differ among themselves on the approach they should adopt toward the policies of the Putin administration. Yabloko has been the most critical of the managed democracy dimensions of the Putin administration policies, which Yabloko leader Grigoriy Yavlinskiy has said threaten to create in Russia a "bureaucratic police state." Union of Right Forces leaders have tried to strike a balance of support and criticism, a policy that recognizes the conflicting patterns of economic and political policies under Putin and the fact that they can claim many of the economic and foreign policies and individual regime officials as their own. Despite strong differences over the proper posture to assume toward the Putin administration, an analysis of voting patterns in the parliament shows highly similar patterns of support by the two parties for the Putin administration's legislative agenda. Both parties have supported key components of the administration's economic and foreign policy agenda while opposing or seeking to water down what they see as antidemocratic elements of its political agenda.[13]

Why Pressures Will Grow for President Putin to Change Course

Many Western analysts see the Putin administration's policies as the harbingers of a new era of authoritarianism in Russia that is likely to be of the "soft" variety but potentially long-lasting. This view is buttressed by what many analysts, inside and outside Russia, assert to be fertile Russian soil, that is, the passiveness of society and the prominence of antidemocratic tendencies in the public as well as the elite. There are good reasons to believe that the political outlook in Russia is far more fluid than the conventional analysis suggests—that the roots of this semi-authoritarian pattern are not deep and its longevity is in doubt.

On the contrary, a closer look at the climate of opinion in Russia's political elite and at the grave challenges facing Russia in the years ahead suggests that the current combination of promarket economic and pro-Western foreign policies with authoritarian drift on the political front is inherently unstable. This unstable amalgam of policies creates the potential for significant change—for President Putin's course to shift in a more assertively authoritarian or a more resolutely democratic direction.

—The attempt to combine free market economic policies with constraints on democracy will not produce the results that President Putin wants. President Putin's first years have been blessed with official statistics showing strong economic growth, one of the factors in his extraordinary popularity. But there is a consensus that this growth has been prompted primarily by fortuitous factors such as the favorable terms of trade prompted by a currency devaluation in 1998 and high prices for Russia's exported oil. Growth rates have already begun to decline. Producing sustained high rates of growth over the longer term will depend increasingly on fundamental structural reforms that reduce corruption and encourage a sharp increase in domestic and foreign investment. The Putin administration has not yet put in place the kind of policies that would show promise of reducing pervasive official corruption. The administration's efforts so far to limit the political influence of Russia's "oligarchs" and insider elites are vulnerable to the charge that he has moved only colectively—against those who have supported the political opposition.[14] The leading anticorruption group Transparency International ranks Russia seventy-ninth of ninety-one countries surveyed, with number one being the "most transparent" or "least corrupt."[15]

The urgency of fundamental reforms beyond what has yet been achieved is underscored by grave problems of human and intellectual capital and economic infrastructure that were inherited from the Soviet era and exacerbated by the economic and social decline of the first post-Soviet decade. Russia suffers from a population declining in numbers and in health and from medical and educational systems that provide care for the majority of the public at the quality more typical of a third world country. These problems threaten Russia's survival as a nation, as President Putin has said, as well as aspirations to restore Russia's place as a great power.[16]

Proponents of an approach to economic and political reform that relies heavily on the state apparatus will increasingly confront the fact that Russia's civil service lacks the professional norms, respect for the rule of law, and relative freedom from corruption that characterize the state-centered approaches followed in some other countries that they hope to emulate. A primary emphasis on political stability and restoring the authority of the central government in Moscow can arguably be seen as a necessary first step in an effort to create strong and effective state institutions. But historical experience suggests that a strategy of massing power in the presidential administration risks impeding the development of strong and autonomous state institutions necessary to the development of an effective state.[17]

Antidemocratic policies will work against the creation of a benign climate for domestic and foreign investment that Putin has made a top priority by restricting the aggressive parliamentary oversight and unfettered press that are necessary to reduce high levels of corruption. Many Russian and American students of Russia's culture and history find it implausible that a policy that seeks to sustain an effort to reduce bureaucracy in the Russian economy can be successfully combined with steps to sustain or increase the bureaucracy's role on the political front.[18]

There are good reasons to doubt that what some have called the "Chilean model" of reform—combining Pinochet-like authoritarianism with free market economic policies—will succeed in the Russian context.

Pinochet's reforms were launched in a country with a long if uneven democratic tradition and with less deeply embedded corruption.

The durability of the political coalition supporting this combination of liberal and authoritarian policies is also suspect. Those in the elite and in Putin's administration who support efforts to shrink the state's role in the economy seem to support the same direction in the political realm. Similarly, Russian analysts suggest that the proponents of managed democracy and an expanded role for the state in the political sphere are proponents of expanding the state's use of administrative regulation and skeptical of the benefits of a deregulated market economy. Every administration has within it different points of view, but the differences within the Putin administration, leading to a situation that some have called "feuding teams," have already led to embarrassing public conflicts over policy and are impeding Putin's effort to set out a coherent course.[19]

Putin's turn toward a more decisive alignment with the West in the wake of September 11 has magnified the apparent contradictions in his political course. The renewed emphasis on integration with the West has widened the gap between the inward and backward looking policies associated with managed democracy and his administration's pro-West and prointegration policies on the economic and national security front. This shift has also solidified support for Putin on the prodemocratic "right" side of Russia's political spectrum and in the West, while prompting increased criticism of the president from those—in the military and security establishment as well as in the Communist Party and from the left side of the political spectrum—who form the core of the political base for managed democracy.

—Committed proponents of managed democracy are confined to a relatively narrow segment of the elite. The data on elite opinion presented in chapter 2 show strong support for democratic values in a cross section of Russia's leaders. This evidence suggests little support for either "hard" or "soft" authoritarianism and certainly no sign that Russia's leadership class as a whole acts as a brake on democratic change. Even within Russia's political elite, the evidence suggests that support for the policies associated with managed democracy is a mile wide but an inch deep. Many centrist politicians seem to support the policies associated with managed democracy because those are the Putin administration's policies, and they see their political livelihood as dependent on the administration. Most of these political figures would support President Putin just as enthusiastically were he to shift to more decisively democratic policies—or to a more authoritarian course.

Russian politicians retain good survival skills learned in the Soviet era. In the current political environment, the signals coming from the top suggest that those leaders who support managed democracy will thrive and those who do not will suffer. Lack of public opposition to controls on political expression can reflect political prudence more than inner conviction.[20]

The political base of the collection of centrist parties that form the core of the support in the parliament for Putin's current course is also fragile. Several previous incarnations of such centrist parties closely wedded to support for administration policies but lacking a clear ideological focus have proved short-lived. The close association of these parties in the public eye with entrenched and often corrupt regional and central elites leaves them vulnerable to challenge from antiestablishment political parties on either the right or the left side of the political spectrum.

Elements of the Russian state bureaucracy constitute a bulwark of support for managed democracy and a relatively authoritarian course. But the Russian government apparatus is hardly monolithic, any more than the American. We can safely assume that the bureaucracy—especially at the middle and lower levels—is staffed with many officials who are willing, and even eager, to carry out new orders from above that adopt a different course from the one currently coming down from the top.

Global experience indicates that the impetus for steps toward deeper democracy has in some cases come from below, that is, from popular pressure against the status quo. In other cases, it has been triggered by divisions within the political elite and the triumph of those who favor democratic change. The original impetus for the dramatic steps toward democratization that ultimately brought down the Soviet Union came from within the Russian political elite, not from people in the street. The breakthrough came when democratic elements at the top of the political structure—in a development that few in the West anticipated—broadened the boundaries of the political arena in an effort to mobilize popular support for their agenda. Under the conditions that Russia faces, this scenario could unfold again.

—Popular support for President Putin's current course is strong but fragile. Public opinion may ultimately serve as another factor impelling President Putin toward a more decisive choice between policies that expand or constrain democratic development in Russia. Putin and his close advisers have made clear that Putin, striving to be the "people's president," closely tracks public opinion polls. Polls suggest his popularity for now remains remarkably high, with between 65 and 75 percent of the population typically expressing confidence in his leadership.

Much of Putin's support rests on factors that increasingly will look transient. This support reflects an appreciation for Putin's vigorous leadership, in the wake of Yeltsin's often absent and inattentive leadership, and for the political stability that has replaced the turbulence of the Yeltsin years. It reflects, as some Russian analysts have suggested, a hope—not necessarily a conviction—that Putin will be able to show the kind of strong leadership needed to forge a consensus on solutions to Russia's problems and the skill and determination to get decisions implemented. Polling results suggest weak support for some of the president's policies, especially ones designed to reduce the state's role in the economy and to trim the size of the state's social safety net—another signal that his high poll numbers may be fragile.

As memories of the Yeltsin years recede, Putin's support will increasingly be based on the results his administration has achieved rather than on hope for what he can accomplish. Opinion surveys make apparent that they will be looking for results that reduce official corruption and improve the economic lot of ordinary citizens. Many Russian political leaders and political pundits, in assessing Putin's first years, fault him for being too cautious and failing to set out a coherent strategy for Russia's further development.[21]

A closer look at the complexion of Putin's popular support base underscores its potentially transient nature. Opinion surveys show respondents who express confidence in Putin's leadership are found about evenly among Russians who identify with parties on the left and right side of the political spectrum as well as among those who identify with no party at all. Supporters on both sides of the spectrum are likely to increasingly look for more resolute support by the president for their own agenda.

Previous post-Soviet Russian politicians, and not just Yeltsin, have emerged onto the political scene with high confidence ratings only to see them subsequently decline precipitously. Studies of presidential popularity in many established democracies indicate that declining ratings commonly occur during a presidential term. While polls show that Putin's confidence ratings remain high, other polls show that most Russians say little improvement in the country's predicament has occurred. Most continue to say that the country is going in the wrong direction.[22]

—Putin's agenda as president ultimately differs from that of any particular government agency or set of political advisers. In Russia's political context (and not only Russia's), the policies pursued by leaders in their first years in power have proved a poor guide to their eventual political direction. The policies pursued by leaders as diverse as Nikita Khrushchev, Leonid Brezhnev, and Mikhail Gorbachev—Boris Yeltsin is an exception—in the first stage of their administrations reflected the dominant interests of the political establishment at the time. All three eventually changed direction.[23] President Putin came to power in a very different, more open context, but both the circumstances of his election and his background in the Soviet intelligence services suggest that he began his public political life with good reasons to reflect the interests of the political establishment.[24]

It is possible, even probable, that Putin will find that his own interests as a leader determined to rebuild the Russian state will diverge from those of the officials who constituted his original support base as he confronts the contradictions between his current course and what is required to ensure his legacy. A respectable historical legacy will not rest on his success in creating political stability, and certainly not on restraining democracy, but on a breakthrough toward the objective he has set of Russia taking a place "consistent with Russia's potential" in the global political and economic arena. Putin's change of course on the foreign policy front in 2001—toward a more decisive alignment with the United States—suggests he is capable of breaking the existing paradigm if he sees it in Russia's and his own interest.

Putin could eventually see the advantages of sharing with judicial and legislative institutions the blame as well as the responsibility for potentially controversial reforms in the planning stages that will reduce the state-supported social safety net. In the same manner, he could find a freewheeling press an ally in fighting the state bureaucracy—whose resistance to change he lamented in his annual address to the Federal Assembly in April 2001—and in confronting the small but relatively influential group of political and economic leaders that seek to preserve the status quo. Alexander Yakovlev, former Soviet leader Gorbachev's closest political adviser, suggests that President Putin's most dangerous enemy will prove to be, not political opposition, but his own bureaucracy.[25] Gorbachev himself went through a transformation during his first years in office—from relying on the state apparatus to concluding that it was the main obstacle—as he struggled to find a path to reform the Soviet system and to find allies who would help him implement reform.

—It is premature to conclude that Putin has yet accumulated the authority and influence in russia's political system to implement his own vision for the country, whatever it may prove to be. Even in established democracies it takes time to consolidate authority, put in place a loyal team, and determine direction. Assessments of Yeltsin's presidency emphasize that deep divisions within the government throughout the 1990s often left government agencies running like independent fiefdoms rather than agents of the president.

Russian analysts underscore how strongly the president relies for advice and support on influential elites—including holdovers from the

Yeltsin administration and former associates from St. Petersburg and the security services—that hold different views on policy issues and form something less than a coordinated team. Russia lacks the legal basis for, and the tradition of, a wholesale turnover of senior officials when a new administration comes to town that would, as in the United States, put in place a (mostly) coherent and loyal team throughout the government.

As acknowledged by a wide range of Russian and American observers, implementing a new policy direction—especially one that is controversial in the power structure—requires not simply signing a new law or decree but successfully putting together a coalition of insiders and influential elites to support the new policy.

Putin's background as a successful bureaucrat rather than a successful politician, and his relatively sudden leap from bureaucracy to national leadership, suggest that his learning curve in the skills of political coalition building is steep. The primary theme of Richard Neustadt, the premier analyst of the American presidency, is the fundamental weakness of the American president, weakness in the sense of the gap between what is expected of the president and the president's ability to carry it through—and the Russian presidency is far from having even those levers of power over government bureaucracy that the American president can rely on. Putin's vigorous efforts to restore power to the Kremlin have reduced the public visibility of influential insiders in the halls of power but it has done little to reduce their political influence.[26]

Putin's popularity does not guarantee him the clout in the Russian system or the loyal lieutenants he needs to implement a political vision that runs against the grain of the establishment. As long as entrenched elites dominate the critical nodes of political power, popularity can protect him against a direct challenge but cannot prevent influential insiders from blocking democratic reforms. But Putin's popularity gives him a potent source of latent political power that he can draw on if he decides to move decisively against those elements in the system who favor the status quo.

These factors suggest considerable fluidity in the current political debate and uncertainty in the Putin administration's future course. A moment of truth may well come in response to renewed decline in economic growth or Putin's popularity, or in response to unpredictable events.[27]

4

Creating a Competitive Political Marketplace

*The central conservative truth is that it is culture, not politics,
that determines the success of a society. The central liberal truth is that
politics can change a culture and save it from itself.*

Daniel Patrick Moynihan

*Economic development makes democracy possible;
political leadership makes it real.*

Samuel Huntington[1]

D evelopments at the grass roots will be decisive in the long term in
shaping Russia's political institutions, but the decisions that Russia's leaders and ruling elites make will be critical in the short term for
facilitating or impeding the development of democracy from the grass
roots. The history of other democratic successes suggests that external
influences and strong leadership can result in rapid and stable democratic development in what had seemed to be an inhospitable
environment. Germany, Italy, and Japan are often cited as examples of
successful democracies that defied earlier predictions that cultural barriers would prevent success. Studies of the success of key countries in
southern Europe and Latin America in moving toward deeper democracy
in the 1970s and 1980s suggest that the policy choices and political skills
of local leaderships were the decisive factor.[2]

In Russia's conditions, it is appropriate for the state to decisively encourage democratic development. Opinion polls show that most Russians

support a paternalistic state that takes the initiative to provide for its citizens. It is consistent with Russian traditions and the pattern that emerged under Yeltsin for the president to play the role of champion of reform.[3] But the pattern of "managed democracy" that began to develop in the last years of Yeltsin's leadership and has dominated so far under Vladimir Putin—through excessive state regulation and manipulation of the rules governing political life—risks discouraging rather than encouraging the growth of democracy from the grass roots.

The experience of other democratic states shows that the Russian government through its policies and actions can help create the conditions necessary for a competitive political marketplace by working toward the establishment of strong political institutions and transparent rules of the game that nourish and support civic activism and citizen involvement. Stimulating democratic development does not require that the government retreat from activism, only that it engage in the right kind of activism. In his study of patterns of civic activism in the United States in the twentieth century, Harvard political scientist Robert Putnam concluded that government initiative stimulated citizen activism, creating what he calls "social capital." Other studies also indicate that, in established democracies, the state was crucial in "enabling, facilitating, and encouraging" the growth of citizen activism.[4]

The greatest impediment to President Putin's stated goal for Russia's future—that it take its rightful place in the world—is the stranglehold on the country's economic and political life of by self-interested leaders in Russia's political and economic system. This elite cannot be dislodged by presidential fiat, new legislation, or additions to the power of the government apparatus to enforce the law. President Putin has created a parliament sufficiently cooperative to pass appropriate laws to reduce corruption and create stronger democratic institutions. In many cases the appropriate legislation is already on the books. The challenge now is to build a political coalition strong enough to challenge this entrenched group by putting into practice the laws that are being passed or are already on the books.

The elements of a political coalition strong enough to challenge the status quo are in place in today's Russia and ready to be mobilized. The data on popular and elite opinion discussed in chapter 2 show that the latent support for new political institutions and deeper democracy is substantial. As already discussed, the economic and social conditions impelling Russia toward deeper democracy are also substantial. The single greatest barrier to the mobilization of the necessary political support for a breakthrough toward deeper democracy is the widespread skepticism in Russian society that the country's entrenched elite can be dislodged.

Leadership by President Putin is the key to dispelling popular cynicism, mobilizing popular support, and creating a coalition for democratic change. The president and the government can put their muscle behind the creation of a more competitive political marketplace that protects and encourages political opposition to Russia's current leaders and the vested interests that surround them.

There is no need to import Western proposals or invent anything new to create such a political marketplace. Proposals for new approaches and institutional changes that would create a democratic breakthrough in Russia are already under discussion by proponents of democratic change. In some cases at least elements of the Putin administration are backing new legislation that heads in the right direction. In some cases new laws and institutions critical to a democratic breakthrough are already on the books, and the remaining challenge is to see that they are effectively implemented.

Nor is there any need to consider changes that would threaten a return to the political turmoil and confrontations of the Yeltsin era. The proposals for democratic change under discussion in Russia today do not call for abrupt changes in direction but instead represent steps that would move Russia's political order incrementally but steadily toward a deeper democracy. They are steps that would support President Putin's objective of building a strong state by building stronger and more effective democratic institutions. They are steps that would be popular with the voting public, responding to the popular disdain for Russia's current political order and the desire for new, more effective institutions.

Proposals for Democratic Change

The president and the administration can make a difference by throwing their weight behind steps now under discussion or already on the books that would

—Augment the power of the parliament to hold the administration and the government apparatus to account;

—Augment the financial and political independence of the judicial branch and its ability to resist corrupt influence by political and business elites;

—Stimulate the creation of a more competitive political party system and a stronger "loyal opposition";

—Put in place stronger safeguards against government manipulation of national and regional elections;

—Strengthen the financial and legal basis for democracy at the grass roots; and

—Strengthen the financial and political framework for a more vigorous, unfettered press.

A Stronger, More Independent Legislative Branch

Russia's legislative branch should have a greater say in forming the government and strengthened authority to oversee government. Members of the upper house should be selected by direct elections.

Like many countries emerging from authoritarianism, Russia is characterized by a political system with a strong presidency and weak legislative and judicial branches. The Soviet legacy of subservient legislatures was reinforced in the post-Soviet era when Yeltsin forced through the 1993 constitution placing the locus of power in the presidency. He was motivated partly by his desire to best a parliament that was determined to block his plans for rapid market reforms.

Proposals to change the constitution to strengthen the legislative branch—shifting powers from the presidency to Russia's Federal Assembly—have been aired repeatedly since the 1993 constitution was approved.[5] They gained political life in the last years of Yeltsin's tenure, garnering support across the political spectrum.

Putin's popularity, the widespread reluctance to take steps that could upset the recent trend toward political stability—and concerns among Russia's proponents of deeper democracy that tampering with the constitution could end up encouraging antidemocratic rather than democratic change—appear for now to have taken the wind out of the sails of proposals for significant constitutional change. Proponents of democratic change have instead begun to focus on a series of initiatives that, without tampering with the constitution, would buttress the authorities of the Federal Assembly.

These initiatives would grant the lower house (the State Duma) the effective authorities for investigating and overseeing the government and the executive branch that it now lacks. They would also expand the legislature's authority to confirm presidential appointees—now limited to the prime minister, the attorney general, and the head of the Central Bank—to include a wider range of government officials.[6]

The changes in the structure of the legislature's upper house that President Putin pushed through in 2000—replacing regional governors and legislature chiefs as ex officio members with members appointed by the governors and regional legislatures—temporarily reduced the stature of that body and its abilities to challenge the administration. But this change has created a new opening to strengthen the independence and authority of the upper house and the parliament rather than weaken it. The changes have stimulated new support from political leaders on the left as well as the right for the idea that the upper house should be directly elected by voters rather than appointed.[7]

Some American and Russian scholars argue that divided government has no precedent in Russian history and little traction in Russia's political culture. Russia's presidentially focused system is the result not of culture and history, however, but of Yeltsin's effort to protect his authority in the early 1990s from an increasingly assertive legislature. Public opinion surveys suggest that—perhaps with memories of Soviet rule fresh in mind—Russian people support the idea of dispersing political power rather than concentrating it in a single institution. Surveys of opinion among deputies in the legislature show that the idea of strengthening the authority of the legislative branch at the expense of the presidency is popular across the political spectrum, including among propresidential parties.[8]

In Russia's current system, the president has decisive influence on any effort to reduce the powers of his office. There are good reasons why Putin and his political advisers could conclude that a stronger and more independent legislature would work to his advantage and to the advantage of his objective of strengthening the authority of the Russian state.

The superpresidential system, in the end, undermined rather than enhanced former president Yeltsin's personal authority and reputation. By failing to divide power and hence responsibility, Yeltsin eventually left office a highly unpopular president, blamed by most Russians for the hardships that the transition away from communism had brought.

Historical experience suggests that superpresidentialism nourishes official corruption owing to the concentration of resources in the hands of the executive branch. A stronger Federal Assembly with credible authority to exercise oversight of government agencies would provide a potent tool to check corruption and encourage responsiveness to presidential decisions.[9]

An Independent Judicial Branch

There is far more political support in the current environment for strengthening Russia's judicial branch than for expanding the powers of the legislative branch. Putin and leaders from the political mainstream, as well as liberal leaders on the right wing, have expressed support for far-reaching reforms to strengthen the judicial branch and enhance its authority and independence. The breadth of support shows that even conservative elements believe a stronger court system is essential to create momentum toward a rule of law and a better climate for business investment.

Russia's two main liberal parties—Yabloko and the Union of Right Forces—have identified judicial reform as one of their top three priorities, along with private property rights and military reform. They see a stronger judicial branch as a means to create stronger protections for individual liberties and a more attractive investment environment.

Historically, Russian courts have been subservient to the executive branch. The inferior role of the courts has been evident in the extensive authorities given to the executive agencies to oversee the courts and by the dependence of court personnel on central and local officials for their livelihood. The 1993 constitution and legislative acts in the early 1990s laid the theoretical framework for a strong court system substantially independent of the other branches of the federal government and local and regional officials.[10]

Reality on the ground has lagged behind the formal legal framework, partly because implementing legislation sometimes stalled in the Yeltsin years. Opinion surveys indicate some recent increase in the public's confidence in the court system, but trust in the courts remains extremely low.

President Putin has called judicial reform his top priority on the political front, and efforts to strengthen the independence of the court system gained new momentum following his election. This new impetus produced its first fruits in the fall of 2001 with the passage of a package of significant reforms. These changes increased the number of judges, dramatically increased judicial salaries, reduced the ability of executive and legislative institutions to influence the selection or decisions of judges, and enhanced the power of the courts in comparison with that of the state prosecutors. The new measures scale back the authorities of the attorney general and law enforcement agencies to oversee and second-guess the decisions of the court and give Russian citizens stronger rights to resist potential infringements of individual rights by law enforcement organizations.[11]

Most liberal politicians would prefer an even more radical package of reforms but, according to one spokesman, the administration's proposals had "85 percent" of what liberals would propose. The changes encountered open resistance from elements of the federal bureaucracy. The attorney general insisted in early 2001 that the reforms were an attempt to copy Western practices that ignored Russian conditions and said they should be postponed until Russian citizens developed greater respect for law.[12]

The new reform package could contribute significantly to enhancing the independence of the court system, protecting individual liberties, and encouraging the rule of law. But strong government constituencies will resist these changes and look for ways to impede them or ignore them. One of the architects of the reform package estimates that 80 percent of the officials in Russia's current legal system openly oppose the reforms.[13] President Putin's strong support will be needed if these measures are to be implemented.

A Stronger, More Competitive Party System

The most important step that President Putin and Russia's current leaders could take toward a competitive political marketplace would be to stimulate the growth of a stronger political party system.

Competitive parties encourage political stability, a goal that in the wake of the instability of the Yeltsin years is highly valued by Moscow political elites and, according to opinion polls, large segments of the population. A stronger party system would also strengthen formal political institutions, diminishing the power of informal networks and personal influence and bringing more of Russia's politics into the public arena. It would have the same effects in Russia's regions, where often the dominance of insider politics is even greater than in Moscow.

With the exception of the Communist Party, with its deep historical roots in the Soviet period, Russia's political parties are Moscow centered, and most of their activity occurs inside the capital's Ring Road. Parties are important in the State Duma, where half the deputies are elected on the basis of a system that features voting for party lists and proportional representation. But there is minimal party presence in the parliament's upper house and in elections in Russia's regions to executive or legislative positions. Neither Yeltsin nor Putin ran for president as a member of a political party, and party affiliation has no place in selection of the prime minister or other leaders of government. Opinion surveys show low levels of party identification across the country.[14]

Russian analysts attribute the superficial nature of Russia's party system to a variety of ills. For one thing, the Soviet Communist Party's legacy gave parties a bad name. Ideology of any stripe has been discredited by Russia's experience with communism, fight against fascism, and hardships brought on by Russia's initial push toward democracy and the market in the 1990s. Decisions made early on by Yeltsin and his team— to craft a system that featured a weak legislature and a dominant executive and to avoid running for president under a party label—contributed to the weakness of Russia's parties.[15] But the factors involved reach beyond Russia's own experience: weak parties with little reach outside the national legislature are typical of developing democracies in their early stages.[16]

There is remarkable consensus across the Russian political spectrum on the need to take steps toward a stronger party system. This consensus has already led, since Putin's election, to significant new legislation designed to stimulate stronger parties with wider reach across Russia.

A new law governing the activity of political parties approved in 2001 is described by its architect, the chairman of Russia's equivalent to the U.S. Federal Election Commission, as designed to create stronger party competition and bring the role played by Russia's parties closer to the role they play in the West. Critics point out provisions for government oversight and regulation of parties that the government could use to control and constrain the growth of those parties it finds objectionable. But the law also includes provisions that the proponents of faster democratic development agree could promote the growth of parties and encourage them to put down deeper roots outside Moscow's Ring Road.

It would require political parties intending to compete for national posts to meet certain minimum requirements for membership in at least half of Russia's regions.[17]

The law has already encouraged a consolidation of Russia's complex party landscape. Parties on the right and in the center have announced initiatives to merge or form associations that would cooperate to run common slates in the next parliamentary elections.

The goal of creating stronger parties led to additional legislation passed in 2002 mandating that half of the seats in all regional legislatures be filled through party list voting beginning in 2003. Legislators from a spectrum of Russia's parties and Putin administration officials back the increase in party list voting as a means to spur the growth of national party infrastructure outside large cities, increase the clout of regional legislatures, check the autocratic tendencies of some regional governors, and bring the insider politics in the regions into the public political arena. A recent study found that party representation in the legislatures of the relatively small number of Russia's regions that already incorporate some party list voting is much higher than in other regional legislatures.[18]

The new legislation has increased discussion in Russia's political circles about additional steps to stimulate party growth. Political figures from the Communist Party, the propresidential centrist parties, and the right-wing parties have suggested that the time is ripe for Russia's government to be formed on the basis of the majority party or majority coalition in the State Duma. This innovation would break sharply with current practice, in which the president names all top government officials with attention to political loyalty and substantive competence but without regard to party affiliation. There are also renewed proposals by political analysts and political party leaders for presidential candidates to run for office in 2004 on the basis of party affiliation and for President Putin himself to join a party.[19]

The proposals for members of the upper house of parliament, the Federation Council, to be chosen through direct election—instead of chosen by regional leaders—would also increase the strength of parties in the Russian political arena.

President Putin, however, faces a dilemma in encouraging stronger parties. Even with safeguards that would allow the administration to attempt to manage the process, in the end stronger parties will mean more competitive politics and more potent opposition to those currently in power. His own remarks about party development betray ambivalence. Putin has said that he favors a larger role for parties and fewer but stronger national parties. But he has equivocated on suggestions that he join a party and that the government be formed on a party basis. Putin has backed both ideas in principle in his public remarks, as good ideas for the time when Russia has a stronger party system that commands more respect from the population, but he has also said that these proposals are premature. He has argued that for now it is best for the president to remain outside the party structure to better represent "all the people." This position puts the president safely in line with public opinion. Solid majorities believe, according to polls, that the president should remain above the partisan political fray.[20]

Joining and leading a political party could be a fairly simple step for Putin to take, but a step that could have a powerful effect on party development. It could also have the effect of forcing Putin to identify himself personally with a more explicit and coherent program for Russia's future development. By identifying himself with a specific program, it could also stimulate the development of a loyal opposition.

A stronger party system could work to Putin's advantage. A party-based government would encourage a more cohesive government of officials subject to some party discipline, an outcome that could assist the president to implement his program. Forming the government on the basis of the parliamentary majority could make it easier for the government to get its legislative agenda adopted. Some Kremlin-connected politicians have recently backed the idea of party government with this goal in mind. Second, stronger parties in the region would place more effective constraints on the tendency of some regional governors and other local leaders to ignore national policies and priorities. This kind of local democracy could serve the administration's objectives of undermining regional fiefdoms, although in a way that would diminish the central government's ability to control events.

Increased Protections against Government Manipulation of Elections

Elections in which voters can make a real choice about who will lead the country are a durable feature of the new Russian political landscape. Polling data support the conclusion of Western analysts that competitive elections are now the only legitimate means to power. But if improving the fairness of the election process is still an important issue in the United States, it remains a far bigger issue in Russia. Current legislation and practice allow the government significant power to influence the results. Especially at the local and regional level, the development of competitive politics and a vigorous opposition has been significantly impeded by the attempts of central and local elites—not always successful—to manage the results of key elections. The potential for such manipulation has grown with the increased influence in the post-Yeltsin era of the proponents of managed democracy, who are uncomfortable with leaving the fate of the Russian state, and their own personal fate, to "a roll of the dice."[21]

Measured against generally accepted yardsticks, international observers gave Russia relatively solid marks for the elections of the 1990s—presidential elections in 1996 and 2000, parliamentary elections in 1993, 1995, and 1999, and a host of regional and local executive and legislative contests. Although fairness issues were recorded, they were judged not to have been systematic and substantial. Those who lost the contests have usually accepted the legitimacy of the results.

International and Russian election watchdog groups identify four primary areas where fairness issues still arise—areas of potential abuse that are not unique to Russia:

—Laws requiring equal access to the media are often violated or ignored. Violations are only sporadically prosecuted. Unequal media access was the most common problem, and arguably the one with the most impact, in the elections of the 1990s.

Box 4-1. *Using the "Administrative Resource"*

The race for governor in the Far East region of Primorye in spring 2001 offers a good case study of the practices, and their uneven record of success, that many Russians link to the government's use of the "administrative resource." Three days before the run-off vote, a regional court disqualified the candidate who had run a strong second to the leader in the first round. The last-minute disqualification opened the way for a Kremlin-backed candidate to be put on the run-off ballot, though the candidate had finished a poor third in the first round. In this case, the court decision was made in spite of the contrary recommendation of the regional election commission. Popular revulsion against the court decision, and against what analysts agreed was a dirty election campaign, was evident as the Kremlin-backed candidate not only lost but came in with fewer votes than "none of the above."

—Legal limits on campaign spending are frequently violated and are not always enforced.

—There are recurring charges of fraud in the counting of ballots, primarily in the local or regional races.

—Government entities at various levels have used their authority over the registration of candidates—or their influence in the courts—to remove candidates that they do not prefer from the ballot, using various pretexts in the language of the election laws.[22]

Individual candidates and private sector organizations are sometimes the apparent perpetrator of these violations. But most often the primary threat to fairness derives from an attempt by either central or regional political authorities to manipulate the results to favor a candidate of its choosing or to protect against an uncomfortable result—what Russians refer to as the use of the "administrative resource."

For the most part, the problem is not a lack of legislation. The legislative framework governing elections and the legislative authority accorded to the government to monitor and regulate the election process have grown over the years. New legislation passed in 1999, before the

1999 Duma and 2000 presidential elections, provided more rights to election observers and required candidates to disclose more details about their income and assets. The issue is more often a concern by Russian and international observers about the government's failure to enforce the laws or tendency to enforce them selectively. As the body of legislation regulating election activity has expanded, the ability of government agencies to find legal pretext for disqualifying political parties or candidates has grown correspondingly.

New legislation passed in 2002 responded in part to recommendations from domestic and international election watchdog groups. They called for additional measures to restrict the ability of government agencies to tilt the playing field to the advantage of candidates they prefer. In the view of many watchdog groups, selective application of election legislation is the greatest threat to free and fair elections in Russia at the present time. Some of these recommendations are as follows:

—Increase the independence of regional and local election commissions. International monitoring groups, including the OSCE, have recommended steps to increase the independence of regional and local commissions from the influence of local governments, who now name some of the members of the commission and often provide office space and other resources critical to their activities. The new 2002 legislation restricts the ability of local governments to unilaterally name commission members.[23]

—Shift more oversight authority to the judicial branch. International election monitoring organizations have expressed concern over the government's use of election laws to refuse to register or to disqualify parties and candidates for their failure to adhere to financial disclosure or other requirements. The 2002 legislation requires that only the courts can make such a decision. Studies indicate that the courts have sided with the government in the vast majority of complaints filed against it by parties or candidates, but the government lost some significant cases in the 1995, 1999, and 2000 legislative elections.[24]

—Strictly enforce campaign finance laws. Government-backed candidates have frequently benefited from selective application of existing legislation limiting expenditures on media advertising and other campaign activities. International election monitoring organizations have called for increasing the relatively low limits on expenditures and stepping up efforts to enforce the new limits.[25]

—Regulate campaign public relations activities more effectively. The Putin government has been considering legislation to give it more authority to restrict improper or illegal campaign public relations activities such as disseminating fabricated stories about opposing candidates. Few Russians deny that this is a serious problem in Russian elections, but some Russian analysts fear that this legislation would only give the government new tools to manipulate the outcome rather than to ensure that it is the result of a free and fair process.[26]

—Monitor elections. Monitoring by nongovernment organizations of election campaigns and the vote tabulation has been a decisive factor in ensuring free and fair elections and preventing government manipulation of the outcome in countries with an authoritarian tradition. In Russia, as in many other countries, monitoring of its first democratic elections was performed primarily by international organizations.[27] Election monitoring by domestic organizations, during the campaign as well as on election day, is on the rise.[28]

Proponents of deeper democracy from Russia's right-wing parties have proposed establishing a public national election monitoring organization independent of the state. Such an organization could unite the efforts of disparate monitoring groups and potentially provide a parallel vote tabulation in national elections, a practice that has worked against government manipulation in a number of other countries, notably in the election that unseated Serbia's Slobodan Milosevic. The Yabloko party has proposed a package of measures to increase the transparency of the government-run vote count that would assist nongovernment organizations to protect against government manipulation.[29]

The presidential administration is widely assumed by many Russian analysts to have been behind the government's use of the "administrative resource" in several regional elections to back favored candidates, but President Putin has said little about free and fair elections so far in his tenure. As the next national elections approach, the posture he assumes will make a difference in whether proponents of managed democracy in the administration are given license to try to manage the elections to achieve a desirable result and whether government agencies assist or hinder the efforts of nongovernment organizations to mount an extensive monitoring effort independent of the state. Strong backing by the president for effective implementation of the new 2002 legislation could significantly reduce the ability of regional leaders to use the "administrative resource."

Strengthened Financial and Legal Basis for Democratic Local Governments

At a minimum, building democratic institutions at the grass roots—at the municipal and local district level—increases the odds of stable democratic development at the national level. A political culture of negotiation and tolerance for opposition and compromise must be learned, and the grass roots is a good place to start. Democratic leaders at the national level are probably better equipped and more effective if they have democratic experience at the grass roots. Some scholars make the case that citizens that have historically been blocked from political participation are most likely to acquire a sense of political efficacy and a conviction that they can affect public policy at the local level. Global experience suggests democracies are strongest when officials at all levels are elected and do not depend too much on central or regional governments for financing their operations. Democratization at the local level does not mean weak central government and in fact can require a strong central government to overcome the resistance of entrenched local authoritarian elites.[30]

There are also conditions unique to Russia that argue for placing a priority on democratic development at the local level. Many Russian and

American scholars would agree that effective governance is impossible under a highly centralized scenario in a country as large and diverse as Russia and lacking a disciplined bureaucracy. Some Russian analysts make the case that encouraging a culture of respect for the rule of law and democratic values should start from the local level. Most Russians still live in mid-sized or smaller cities or in rural areas where their direct contact is primarily with local government institutions.[31]

As at the national level, democracy at the grass roots took some big steps forward as the USSR collapsed. Local legislative organs were chosen through real, competitive elections for the first time in 1990. The new Russian constitution adopted in 1993 gave explicit backing to the independence of local governments. Legislation backed by the Yeltsin administration provided additional elements of a formal framework for strengthening independent, democratic institutions at the local level. The democratic impetus stalled by the mid-1990s, however, at the local level as well as in Moscow, as the principle of democratic local government was subordinated to political power struggles. Independent local government met fierce resistance from central government ministries and from governments at the regional level. This reverse trend was encouraged by Yeltsin as he sought to increase executive authority at the center and in the process gave regional governors the right to appoint local government executives.[32]

Yeltsin's support for independent local government waxed and waned, but by the end of the Yeltsin era progress had stalled. Local executives remained under the thumb of regional governors. With the key resource decisions dependent on the local executive's ability to strike deals with the regional governor, local legislatures remained relatively powerless, subordinate to local executives. Most Russian and Western analysts place primary responsibility for this stalemate on the failure of the Russian leadership under Yeltsin to give the development of democratic local government a high priority and in particular on its failure to provide local governments with a reliable source of revenue, leaving them to plead for resources from regional governors and from Moscow.[33]

The leaders of Russia's liberal parties have argued that strengthening local government should be a critical dimension of efforts to rebuild the state and have included legislation to do so as part of their political programs. Liberal politicians, supported by local leaders and in some cases by political leaders in the centrist parties or on the left, are discussing initiatives to more clearly delineate the authorities of local government, and they stress the importance of a dedicated revenue source for local governments. Russia's decision to sign onto a European Union convention on local self-government seems to be providing an impetus to this discussion.[34]

President Putin's position remains elusive. In his early remarks Putin alluded to Russia's traditions as a "supercentralized state." Early initiatives from his administration, including a reduction of the proportion of tax revenue alloted to local government, worked against independent and democratic local government. Some analysts concluded that the Putin administration was prepared to forgo federalism in favor of a "unitary state."[35]

More recently, Putin has publicly spoken in favor of strengthening the financial independence of local government, although he has not committed himself to any specific initiatives that would advance local democracy. In meetings with government officials in early 2001, Putin suggested he would support steps to increase the proportion of federal revenue channeled to local governments and otherwise strengthen their financial base. In June 2001 Putin issued a decree setting up a working group to develop proposals for defining the proper division of authorities among the federal, regional, and local governments. This effort is headed by a deputy chief of the Presidential Administration, who also headed up the working group that developed the relatively liberal package of proposals for judicial reform presented to the Duma and voted into law in 2001.[36]

In this instance as in others, Putin could find that his goals are better served by more democracy at the grass roots rather than less: some Russian analysts have suggested that strong local governments could serve as allies of the center in resisting excessive powers and separatist tendencies by regional governors.[37]

An Invigorated Russian Press

Democracies have been more successful than other political systems in creating conditions for economic progress and social justice owing to reliable protections for an unfettered press that is willing and able to challenge vested interests. An unfettered press is essential to muster the information and political support that successful states need to identify mistakes, make corrections, and create the basis for sustained economic and political growth. Independent media have been critical in stimulating pluralism and democratic institutions in other new democracies, such as the former communist countries of central Europe.[38]

The last years under Gorbachev and the first years under Yeltsin saw bold steps by Russian leaders to lay the structural framework for an unfettered press. Freedom of the press is a key tenet in the 1993 constitution.[39] Supporters of democratic change scored a major victory with the successful passage of a law on the press in 1991 that prohibits prior restraint and establishes the legislative base for substantial freedoms. As a result of these new freedoms, the number and national impact of media organs independent of the state grew steadily through most of the 1990s.[40]

Despite these legal advances, even nominally independent media in Russia have remained vulnerable to pressure from the state for political and economic reasons. Even the liberal 1991 press law includes provisions requiring that media organizations be registered and licensed by the state and allows the state to shut them down under certain conditions. Many media legally independent of the state remain economically dependent because of the government's control of printing presses, paper and electricity supply, broadcast frequency, and means of distribution. Many continue to receive direct subsidies from the state owing to the difficulty of achieving financial independence on the basis of advertising and subscription revenue alone. Subscriptions to Russian newspapers have declined as costs have risen closer to market values. Advertising revenues, already meager because of Russia's financial straits, were devastated by the financial crisis that followed the 1998 devaluation of the ruble. One Russian estimate suggests that advertising covers only an average of 20 percent of the costs of mass media publications in Russia, compared with around 80 percent in the United States.[41] Some media organizations have left themselves open to political pressure through poor fiscal management and by failing to maintain high professional standards.

Under Yeltsin, the state employed a light hand in exploiting these financial and political vulnerabilities. The Yeltsin administration used its muscle to encourage positive coverage of the president and his political allies, especially during election campaigns, and negative coverage of his opponents. Media in the regions, partly because of the absence of the wealthy business oligarchs who provided alternative funding to some central media, were even more vulnerable to political pressure from regional governors.[42]

This pattern of state pressure on independent media has accelerated under President Putin. A climate conducive to state control was established by the September 2000 Information Security Doctrine, which places media freedoms in the context of protecting the state's national security interests. A pattern of harassment of national-level media that have been the most outspoken in criticizing Putin and his government— carried out by tax and law enforcement agencies or state-controlled private entities such as the gas monopoly *Gazprom*—has inspired similar behavior by political leaders in Russia's regions. Many Russians speak of a new climate of fear that deters candid reporting about official wrongdoing.

Most of those who worry about freedom of the press in Russia would agree that a stronger economy—by increasing the advertising and subscription market—will be the main engine for an unfettered press in the long term. But legislators from Russia's right-wing parties and other proponents of faster democratic change have also proposed steps that could make a difference in the near term. They have proposed measures that would

—Prohibit any firm or individual—including state-dominated firms such as *Gazprom*—from owning more than a relatively small proportion of any media outlet;

—Provide tax advantages for media advertising expenses;

—Shift responsibility for regulatory oversight from a government ministry to an autonomous agency separate from the executive branch;

—Create a financial fund to support journalists in the central media who lose their jobs for political reasons.

Representatives of nongovernment organizations working with Russian media are convinced that, even working within the existing legal framework, many independent Russia media organizations could increase their financial well-being through better business practices and catering more effectively to a sizable reading public interested in fact-based reporting and more professional journalism.[43]

Through their rhetoric and sometimes through actions, President Putin and his government have occasionally supported a free press. Putin has many times formally expressed his support for freedom of the press. He has been quoted as expressing concern about government-dominated businesses holding an ownership share in media companies. Government spokespersons have opposed draft legislation that would limit the television air time that could be devoted to advertising and supported amendments that narrowed the reach of proposed legislation restricting foreign ownership of Russian media organizations. In remarks to American journalists following his summit meeting with President Bush in June 2001, Putin said the most important factor in establishing a free press was to create the necessary "economic base," and he insisted that the government, and he personally, had set themselves this task.

Through both actions and by lack of action, however, the thrust of Putin's policy so far has been to support a gradual erosion of press freedom. Whether or not he pulled the strings in the takeover of Russia's most influential national television channels by state-influenced entities in 2001 and 2002, in public he stood aside from the fray. He has passed up the opportunity afforded by these controversial moves to send a clear signal in public remarks that an independent press prepared to express opposition viewpoints is a high priority for Russia's development. Most of Putin's public comments have suggested that the threat to press freedom comes from monopoly control by Russia's business oligarchs rather than from the state. By failing to give the objective of an independent and unfettered press more priority, and by condoning or accepting the pattern of government harassment of media outlets, the president has so far provided political cover for federal ministries and regional leaders looking for an excuse to restrain or suppress independent media.

The most potent step President Putin could take to stimulate an unfettered press would be to change the signals that he and senior government officials are sending through their actions at the top. Were he to treat an unfettered press as an ally in his quest to build a strong Russian state, rather than as a threat, Putin could quickly change the climate that has encouraged harassment of independent journalists by lower-level officials at the national and regional level. One way to do that would be to abolish the government's press ministry or transform it into a regulatory body independent of the executive branch.

The president could also follow through on his pledge to support steps to strengthen the financial base for independent media. A Putin administration working group is reportedly weighing amendments to the 1991 press law that would stimulate the advertising market and restrict the ability of the state or individual businesses to acquire control of major media enterprises. Right-wing political parties and journalist organizations back the legislation.

Putin's Dilemma: Deeper Democracy or a Turn toward Stagnation?

There is a powerful impetus in the Russian elite, supported by public opinion, to restore Russia's status as a great state, capable of providing prosperity for its citizens and worthy of global influence. Achieving that goal will require the creation of strong and durable democratic institutions. Especially in a state that is the size and complexity of the Russian Federation, such institutions can not be created by presidential edict or central government regulation. But government activism—by stimulating the development of stronger political and civil society institutions—can make a difference in how fast and how far Russia advances in a democratic direction.

The era of dramatic institutional change and political transformation in the new Russia seems to be over. But in its wake is widespread recognition that the Yeltsin era failed to complete the construction of the necessary institutional basis for a modern democratic state and that more political change, of the incremental variety, is needed. No one, other than a handful of insiders, is happy with the status quo bequeathed by the Yeltsin era. As the evidence in this chapter suggests, there is lively discussion in the Russian elite about additional institutional change that could produce progress toward a more vigorous democratic order. No one is proposing sweeping changes that would replace the current political order. But many government officials and analysts are discussing proposals in individual areas—with significant potential impact on the parliament, the courts, and the party system—that together amount to an ambitious agenda for change.

These debates about change could come to naught, as many did in the Yeltsin era. But the undercurrent of support in Russian society for measures that will make Russia a more prosperous and just society and the Putin administration's apparent appreciation for the value of strong state institutions—suggests that it would be a mistake to assume that stagnation will again be the outcome.

Through their influential positions in the government and private business, insiders will seek to water down and block the initiatives currently being discussed or to impede their implementation even if they are adopted. President Putin's position will be decisive in determining whether they are successful. Far more than Yeltsin, Putin has the bureaucratic savvy, personal discipline, and popular support needed to confront and overcome this kind of resistance.

Putin's origins are in the conservative elements of the elite, many of whom appear to see pluralism and democracy as more of a threat to the Russian state than an opportunity. In his first months and years, he has supported policies that reflect that mind-set. But the test of Putin's leadership is still to come.

Only bolder moves toward pluralistic institutions have the potential to make real progress against the inertia and corruption that stand in the way of Russia's path to a great state. This reality is likely to become increasingly apparent to Putin and his administration if it is not already. The true test of leadership will be his willingness to confront the status quo inclinations of his erstwhile allies and put the weight of his office and strong popularity ratings behind an effort to ensure progress. Russia must move toward a more competitive political marketplace where political opposition is seen not as a threat but as a necessary ingredient of a great state.

5

America's Ability
to Make a Difference

The United States cannot afford to stand on the sidelines; you cannot be an outside observer.

Soviet foreign minister Eduard Shevardnadze to
U.S. secretary of state James Baker, 1991[1]

The reorientation of Russia's foreign policy toward faster integration with the West following the terrorist attacks of September 11 has transformed Russia's debate about democratic development. An environment far more conducive than before to a breakthrough toward deeper democracy now prevails. A shift toward a U.S.-Russia relationship based on shared values and shared tactical interests seems more conceivable than at any time since the first months after the collapse of communism and the rise to power of prodemocratic forces. Consummating this potential alliance depends on profound changes in Russia's political order toward stronger democratic institutions and behavior. But America's policy toward Russia will be crucial in determining whether the forces in Russia who seek such change succeed.

The U.S. Potential and Russia's Democratic Development

The United States should not seek to impose Western institutions on Russia's political landscape or lecture Russian leaders about shortcomings in their current democratic practice. Instead, by the way it shapes its foreign policies, and policies toward Russia in particular, the United States can influence the unfolding of Russia's internal debate. A close look at the history of U.S.-Russian relations and at the role that U.S. policy plays in the current Russian political scene demonstrates the following:

—The United States can profoundly affect the debate in Russia's political elite about democratic development;

—The United States has more influence than ever before in the wake of the terrorist acts of September 11;

—The most important step the United States can take is to demonstrate that it supports Russia's desire to be a strong and great state;

—Treating Russia as part of the West rather than as a country whose choice is still to be made can become a self-fulfilling prophecy; and

—Seeking Russia's accelerated integration into Western institutions creates the right environment for a dialogue about standards of democratic behavior that all members are expected to meet.

U.S. policy should acknowledge that the impediment to deeper democracy in Russia is a relatively small group of self-interested elites—whose influence is vulnerable to attack—and not the Russian public, President Vladimir Putin, or the predominant portion of Russia's political and economic leaders.

The most important democratic value that the United States can support is the creation of a more competitive political marketplace in Russia, established through measures that will buttress the independence and vigor of Russia's legislative and judicial branches of government, create a more competitive system of political parties, and stimulate and protect a robust, free press.

U.S. Influence in Historical Perspective

During the past three decades the breadth of U.S. engagement with Russian leaders on issues of democracy and individual liberty has expanded along with a greater emphasis in U.S. foreign policy on promoting democracy abroad. Just how large a role to accord internal issues in bilateral dealings with Russia and America's other diplomatic partners remains a matter of debate. But, globally, the idea that seeking to engage other countries in a dialogue on democracy and other internal policies constitutes an inappropriate "interference in internal affairs" has gradually lost weight since the 1970s. International treaties and conventions have increasingly focused on human rights and democracy, as well as economics, regional issues, and arms control.[2]

Since the 1970s, U.S. officials have engaged Russian leaders from Leonid Brezhnev to Putin on subjects ranging from individual liberties and freedom of emigration to general principles of democracy. Russian leaders have sometimes bridled at U.S. interventions on internal issues, but the importance of the U.S. relationship to Russia's global aspirations has impelled them to engage on these issues and often to respond.[3]

American leaders' initial exchanges on democratic values with Russian leaders in the 1970s were narrowly focused and highly adversarial. Soviet leaders stepped up repression of political dissidents in the face of the Carter administration's expressions of concern about their treatment. Foreign Minister Andrey Gromyko's response when Secretary of State George Shultz raised human rights issues such as treatment of dissidents and freedom of emigration in the early 1980s was to disparage it as a "tenth rate question" not worthy of high-level diplomacy.[4]

In the late 1980s Soviet leader Mikhail Gorbachev's turn toward liberalization gradually opened the way to a drastic change in the tone of the bilateral encounters. By the late 1980s, there was dialogue and give-and-take in private meetings with Gorbachev and top Soviet leaders, and the subject of internal change was treated as a legitimate subject for discussion.[5] By the end of the second Reagan administration, the president and secretary of state were discussing internal issues in Russia in regular meetings with Gorbachev and Foreign Minister Eduard Shevardnadze, as U.S. officials sought to encourage Gorbachev's moves toward openness and democratization and to make the case that democratization was in the Soviet Union's national interest.

Persistent U.S. efforts to influence and support democratic change in Russia have, over time, brought results. Even during the early years, when Soviet leaders bridled at American hubris, in many cases they ultimately responded with concessions on specific human rights cases. Gorbachev told Secretary of State Shultz that their extended conversations on democracy and openness had influenced the policies that his administration adopted. The decision of U.S. and other Western leaders to withhold support for the government installed by the 1991 coup against Gorbachev contributed to its early demise. Former Clinton administration officials believe American interventions on select occasions in the 1990s were influential, if not decisive, in deflecting potential anticonstitutional steps by the Yeltsin administration against its political opposition.

Growing American Influence

Even before September 11, America's ability to influence Russian developments was regularly underestimated. Opinion polls show that most members of the Russian elite see movement toward a market economy, Western-style institutions, and closer integration with Europe as Russia's only path to a prosperous future. Putin and his team from the beginning of their tenure associated themselves with this view. Moscow political insiders are wary of U.S. tutorials, but they view U.S. and Western investment as critical for renewed economic growth. Russian officials want to be part of Europe, but they see relations with the United States as central to fulfilling their aspirations for a global diplomatic role for Russia.

Despite the cooling of U.S.-Russian ties during the 1990s and increasing skepticism about U.S. intentions, moreover, opinion surveys show that the Russian public continued to support closer ties. Large majorities,

even though gloomy about U.S. intentions, said they wanted closer cooperation. Polls in early 2000 showed overwhelming majorities of Russian
citizens supporting closer ties with the West and rejecting the option of
"distancing" Russia from the West. Other polls indicate strong popular
support for efforts by the Russian government to restore the country's
status as a great power but little or no support for efforts to position Russia as a counterweight to the United States as a means to achieve that
objective.[6]

The shift in Russian policy following September 11 has created a new
political context, so that U.S. policy choices will have even greater reverberations within Russia's political leadership. The policy shift commits
Russia more decisively to a thoroughgoing integration with Western
institutions, reaffirms the centrality of the United States in Russia's relations with the West, and further erodes the notion that Russia might
seek to draw closer to Europe while keeping its distance from the United
States. Russia's reorientation creates the potential for a growing web of
relations with the West.

Targeting an Entrenched but Vulnerable Elite

U.S. policy should be based on the premise that the main impediment to
deeper democracy is a small but well-entrenched segment of Russia's
elite—not the Russian public and not President Putin. The data show
that—with enlightened leadership—movement toward deeper democracy is possible and even probable in current Russian conditions. Most
Russians want to create stronger democratic institutions and will respond
to democratic leadership.

The Russian political elite is no more united in its views—including
on the subject of deeper democracy—than the American political elite.
The main impediment to movement toward democracy is a segment of
influential elites that is well positioned but nonetheless only a segment.
Those groups who support the status quo and resist democratic change
are the same ones who resist President Putin's shift toward strategic
alignment with the United States. The United States, through its choice

of policies, can create a political context in Russia that discredits these elites and buttresses the position of leaders who seek deeper democracy. The robust size of the political center in Russia, populated by parties and politicians with no clear ideological commitment, adds to the impression of potential fluidity.

It would be a mistake for the United States to approach President Putin personally as the obstacle to deeper democracy. Some Western assessments of Putin are profoundly pessimistic. They argue that Putin, as a product of his KGB background, has already made clear that his bias for order and distaste for opposition, along with his strong popular support, leave him with no understanding of democratic values and no taste for giving them priority on the Russian policy agenda. Most of those who take this view would also argue that Putin should be seen as personally responsible for the antidemocratic actions that elements of his government have initiated, such as harassing media organizations, journalists, environmental activists, and others who have shown excessive zeal in opposing the government.

Western observers have often overestimated the personal power of Russian (and American) presidents and their direct responsibility for any activity by the Russian government. They have often overestimated the cohesion within the Russian government and underestimated the degree to which individual agencies and political actors may act on their own. They have underestimated the complexities of presidential power and the difficulty of building political coalitions to support controversial changes. They have frequently failed to anticipate how much the policies of presidents—such as former Soviet leader Gorbachev—can evolve.

Whatever the West's private calculations about Putin's personal responsibility for antidemocratic actions and commitment to the democratic values he has publicly espoused, U.S. diplomacy should be constructed to encourage him to act on his promises to builder deeper democracy. U.S. leaders should recognize that undermining the position and the policies of a well-entrenched elite demands more than a day and more than a handful of presidential decrees.

Supporting Russia's Desire for Greatness

The most important step America can take to bolster Russia's democratic development is to pursue policies that support Russia's desire to be a great state. The failure of Russia's effort to build a stronger democracy in the 1990s was in part the result of the steadily increasing political influence of antidemocratic and anti-Western elites throughout the decade. Their increased influence was facilitated by American policies that were seen in Russia as designed to take advantage of Russia's weakness and to expand U.S. influence.

Results from early public opinion polls in the last years of Gorbachev and the first year of the Yeltsin era suggest that the Russian people and the elite were eager to create what they thought of as Western-style institutions. Opinion surveys showed that more Russians than not in the immediate wake of the collapse of communism said that the United States should help build democracy in Russia.[7] Opinion surveys in the early 1990s showed that large majorities of Russians held favorable views of the United States.

The significant decline in economic and social conditions through the 1990s, together with shifting perceptions of U.S. policies, brought a gradual decline in support for Western assistance and a negative slide in attitudes toward the United States. Polling data indicate that by the end of the 1990s solid majorities of Russian citizens said that the intention of the United States during this period was to weaken Russia rather than to assist it to create a strong and vibrant market democracy. By 1995, 59 percent of Russians said that the United States was seeking to exploit Russia's weakness, according to polling data, and by 2000 that share had risen to 81 percent (see figures 5-1 and 5-2). In a poll in October 2000, more Russians (41 percent) described the United States as unfriendly than friendly (33 percent). By comparison, 45 percent of Russians viewed Germany as friendly and only 18 percent as unfriendly.

Two factors seem to have triggered this shift in sentiment. Many Russian citizens attribute the hardships they have suffered to what they see as the leadership's attempt to create Western-style institutions or at least to

Figure 5-1. *Shifting Opinion of the United States*[a]

Percent

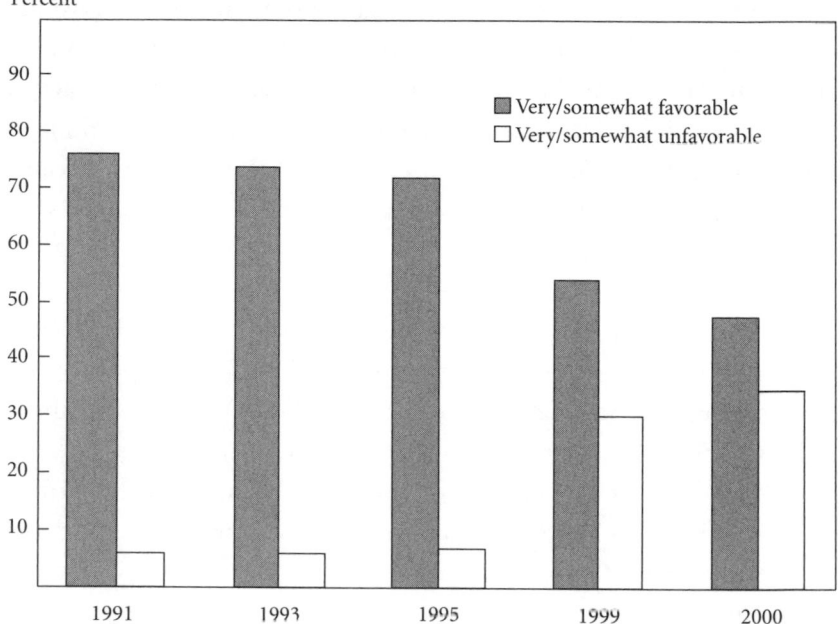

Source: Richard B. Dobson, "Is Russia Turning the Corner? Changing Russian Public Opinion, 1991–1996," Research Report R-7-96 (USIA, Office of Research and Media Reaction, September 1996); Department of State, Office of Research, "Russians' Mistrust of the U.S. at New High," Opinion Analysis M-30-00 (March 14, 2000).

a. "Would you say that your opinion of the United States is very favorable, somewhat favorable, somewhat unfavorable, or very unfavorable?"

install them in a way insufficiently sensitive to Russian conditions and social justice. These efforts were widely seen as redounding to the benefit of a small, privileged group at the expense of ordinary citizens. At the same time, polling data suggest that American foreign policies—such as the enlargement of the North Atlantic Treaty Organization (NATO) to the East and the American effort to encourage options for the export of Caspian basin energy that bypassed Russia and Russia's fuel sector—contributed to the sentiment that American policy was intended to exploit Russia's weakness.

The skepticism of ordinary Russians reflects disappointed expectations. Many Russians, having discarded the communist regime, expected massive Western assistance and a warm welcome into the West and the

Figure 5-2. *Growing Suspicion of U.S. Intentions*[a]

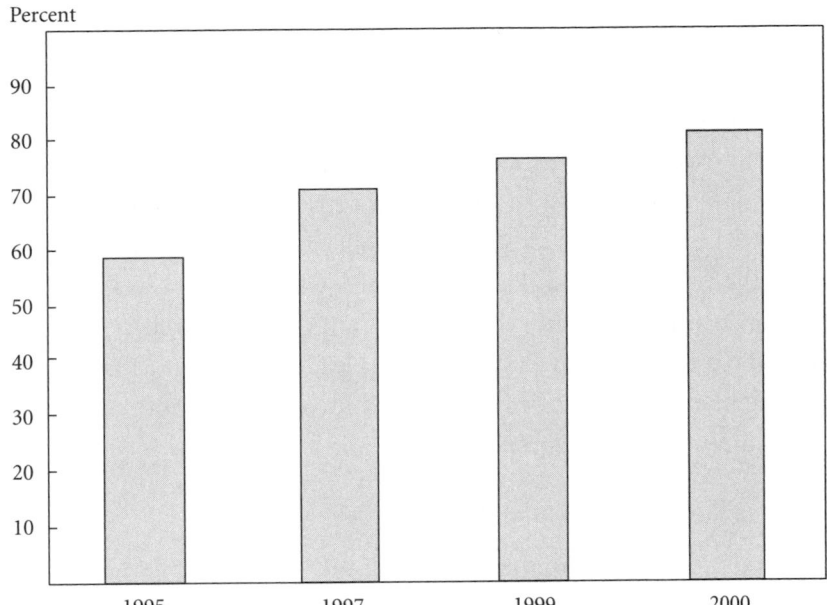

Percent

Source: Department of State, "Russians' Mistrust of the U.S. at New High."
a. "The United States is utilizing Russia's current weakness to reduce it to a second-rate power and producer of raw materials." Figure shows percent who agree with this statement.

community of nations. Western assistance and foreign direct investment failed to meet those expectations. Many Russians saw the decision to expand NATO to include former communist states in central Europe but not Russia as a sign that their country was being left out of emerging postcommunist security structures in Europe. A driving factor appeared to be not facilitating Russia's participation in Western security institutions, but offering Russia's neighbors insurance against the possibility that any effort to integrate Russia would fail.[8]

These sentiments made it easier for anti-American elements in the ruling elite to argue that the Gorbachev and Yeltsin leaderships had made too many concessions to U.S. demands and that U.S. policy was meant to weaken, not strengthen, Russia.

Anti-Western elements in the elite have been making remarkably similar comments about President Putin's policies in the wake of his reorientation of policy toward the United States after September 11. They argue that Putin's concessions to the United States—on a new strategic arms agreement and on the end of the Anti-Ballistic Missile Treaty, and his support for U.S. military activity in former Soviet states along Russia's southern border—have not been reciprocated and reflect a U.S. desire to reduce Russia's role in the international arena.

Russian leaders across the political spectrum want to restore Russia's ability to be a global player. American policies that demonstrably undermine the argument that the United States wants to weaken Russia will help undermine the political position of antidemocratic elements in the elite who push it most avidly and support leaders who argue that a strategic alignment with the United States is Russia's best route to restored credibility as a global player.[9]

Treating Russia as Part of the West

Treating Russia as part of the West rather than as a country whose choice is still to be made can become a self-fulfilling prophecy. Putin's reorientation of Russian foreign policy after September 11 reflects his apparent conviction that Russia's most promising path to modernization and a global role worthy of its traditions is through integration with Western institutions. Until September 11 at least, this was the point of view of only a distinct minority of Russia's most pro-West, prodemocratic elite. Others, more skeptical of the West and hostile to Western values, saw and continue to see Russia's optimum route to greatness in an effort to position Russia as a counterweight to American global prominence and a beacon to those countries that bridle at what they see as a U.S. aspiration to dominance and bent for unilateralism.

The United States, through its policies toward Russia's integration, will influence the outcome of this debate. The United States has rhetorically supported Russia's integration into Western institutions since the rebirth of the Russian state following the collapse of communism. But that rhetorical commitment has not always driven American policy. Many Russians perceived some U.S. policies in the 1990s as intended to isolate rather than to include Russia in the Western family of nations.

Making it clear that U.S. support for Russia's gradual integration with the West is not just rhetoric but an essential feature of American strategy will strengthen the hand of those leaders in the government and others who support the sometimes controversial policies needed to prepare Russia for deeper integration. Policies and statements from the United States that can be interpreted as signaling that the U.S. support for Russian integration is hollow rhetoric will have the opposite effect. Anti-American elements in the Russian elite will seize any pretext to make their case that Russia is not welcome in the West. Some prominent Russian prodemocracy politicians assert that, with domestic opposition to potential authoritarian drift relatively weak, Russia's broadening integration into the West is the only way such drift can be checked.[10]

Treating Russia as part of the West rather than as a state whose strategic orientation remains in doubt can powerfully affect the pace of its moves toward deeper democracy. Studies of efforts to build democracy in the postcommunist world in eastern and central Europe during the 1990s indicate that geographical proximity to western Europe—and with it the real prospect of joining European institutions—may be the most important factor creating a democratic pull. The United States and its European allies can accelerate Russia's democratic trajectory by creating an environment in which Russia is *virtually* proximate to western Europe and its institutions.[11]

Russia is a candidate for integration in some way and at an appropriate time into various Western-based multilateral institutions, such as the Organization for Economic Cooperation and Development, the European Union, the Group of Seven leading industrialized democracies that make up the G-7, the Council of Europe, and NATO. But Russia's relationship with NATO will for the near term be seen by many in Russia and the West as the litmus test of the prospects for Russia's integration into the West. Integration into the European Union appears to be an issue of the far distant future for Russia. Many American and Russian analysts believe that it will be easier to integrate Russia into common security structures such as NATO than into the European Union.[12] Russia's status in and with NATO will have particular resonance in Russian domestic politics.

Convincing Russia that the West seeks its inclusion rather than isolation from Europe's leading security organization will have a larger impact than any other step on Russia's governing elites. The creation in May 2002 of the NATO-Russia Council is a move in the right direction. The council gives Russia a seat at the NATO table on certain issues although without a member's veto power on any of them.[13]

There are good reasons why it is in the U.S. national interest to move forward now with initiatives that will make the council a real decision-making body and create a framework that anticipates Russia's full membership in the alliance. Increasingly, the security challenges facing NATO and Russia—such as global terrorism—are compatible or identical. The prospect of membership in NATO has powerfully affected candidate countries in central Europe, giving them an impetus toward stronger democracy and propelling new, more democratically and Western-oriented officials into the ranks of their governments. The prospect of NATO membership could produce the same results in Russia. Some accounts of Russia's internal debates over the first phase of NATO enlargement in the mid-1990s suggest that those officials arguing for a more robust Russian involvement with the alliance were undercut by evident hostility in the West to the idea of Russia's incorporation.[14]

A convincing strategy for Russia's integration into NATO will mean creating specific mechanisms and an agreed-on road map for Russia's entry and a willingness to accept basic changes in the nature of the alliance. It does not mean belittling the obstacles that remain or offering Russia any special advantages.

Creating a Bilateral Dialogue on Democracy

Seeking Russia's accelerated integration into Western institutions creates the right environment for a dialogue with Russia's leaders on standards of democratic behavior that all members are expected to meet. The controversial results of U.S. efforts to support Russian democracy and influence the country's internal transformation in the 1990s have led to suggestions that it is futile or counterproductive to try to influence the decisions of Russia's leaders about the course they should take. There are lessons to be learned from the experience of the 1990s. But the lesson is not that the United States should not engage, only that the way in which America engages makes a difference.

Russians who support democratic change would concur that it is counterproductive for the United States to offer advice on specific policies or U.S. backing to those leaders who support such policies. Supporting democracy does not mean exporting American institutions. But most of Russia's own proponents of democratic change would argue against the notion that the West should treat Russia's progress toward a deeper democracy as a strictly internal affair.

Russians who are working at the cutting edge of democratic change and most vulnerable to pressures from antidemocratic forces in the federal or regional governments say that a U.S. retreat from engagement will be interpreted by opponents of democratic development as a green light for harassment.[15] An agenda for U.S.-Russian relations released on the eve of the first meeting between presidents Bush and Putin in June 2001 by the Russia–U.S. Association—a collection of important Russian political analysts and former government officials—proposed that Russia's democratic development and integration into the West be prominent issues on the U.S.-Russia bilateral agenda.[16] With internal opponents of authoritarian drift weakened by the government's moves against independent voices, the international community's voice will be even more important.

Creating a credible conviction in Moscow that Russia's integration into the West is a priority for the United States creates the right environment for Western governments to raise potentially sensitive issues about Russia's internal political development. Placing, for example, media freedoms, human rights, and rule of law in the context of a strategy for Russia's integration into the West puts these issues clearly in the context of Russia's national interests rather than as subjects that serve only America's parochial interests.

History again suggests the effectiveness of this approach. To an extent not appreciated by the West or the Soviet leadership at the time, the commitments to human rights that the Soviet Union signed in 1975 at the Helsinki Conference on Security and Cooperation in Europe subsequently provided a useful framework for both internal proponents of liberalization and Western governments to engage Soviet leaders on human rights issues.

—The United States should consider establishing a dialogue on democracy issues under the umbrella of working groups that discuss formal criteria for Russia's path toward membership in Western and other multilateral institutions. This context would underscore American and Western support for Russia's integration into Western institutions, and in the government's internal deliberations would allow Russian officials open to a dialogue on democracy issues to outflank those participants who oppose such a dialogue.

—The most productive engagement on sensitive topics often comes from relatively small and informal private diplomatic exchanges rather than from exchanges of public rhetoric, in the same manner that many issues from human rights to official corruption have been handled in the past.

Making democracy issues a central and visible part of the bilateral dialogue need not impede cooperation on counterterrorism or other urgent security and regional issues if the discussion takes place in a context of encouraging Russia's accelerated integration into Western institutions. Establishing a pattern of regular bilateral engagement that includes all these issues allows both sides to accept that a productive relationship on one front encourages progress on the others. It does not make cooperation on security and counterterrorism contingent on steps toward deeper democracy. Since the 1970s the record shows that any attempt to link Russian behavior on democracy issues more explicitly to other issues in the bilateral relationship is counterproductive.[17]

A common approach with U.S. allies in Europe will be more effective than a unilateral approach. Integration with European institutions is far less controversial in the Russian elite than integration with the United States. Similarly, it is easier for many Russians to listen to European advice.

The United States may need to take the lead in facilitating a common approach to democracy issues. Some European leaders have shown a willingness to broach issues of democracy and human rights with Putin administration officials while others have held back. The ability of the United States to have an impact will be undermined if the message is not shared widely in the alliance and repeated with conviction.

Building a Personal Relationship between Presidents

American diplomats have come away from their careers of engaging Russian leaders convinced that building credible personal relationships is sometimes the best way to wield U.S. influence on difficult issues, both on the foreign and domestic policy fronts. Personal diplomacy at the summit level was decisive in resolving controversial issues during the tenure of former Soviet leader Gorbachev and his predecessors. Personal accounts of the participants convey a conviction that U.S. objectives to move Russia's internal policies were more effectively advanced if the most sensitive issues and sharpest criticisms were broached primarily or initially through channels of personal diplomacy.

The end of the Soviet era did not diminish the value of personal relationships at the top level. Former deputy secretary of state Strobe Talbott describes steady, constant personal diplomacy—especially between Presidents Clinton and Yeltsin—as the primary mechanism that facilitated the successful resolution of residual contentious issues in the relationship left over from the collapse of the Soviet Union.[18]

Private exchanges at the top level were an essential feature in the Clinton administration's approach to what it saw as one of its key objectives—keeping Russian democracy on track. The most important issue of internal policy in private exchanges with President Yeltsin was a U.S. concern that Yeltsin, in his political battles with opponents, stay within the bounds of the Russian constitution and in particular that his administration proceed on schedule with presidential and parliamentary elections. Throughout the 1990s, notably during the electoral race between Yeltsin and communist leader Gennadiy Zyuganov in 1996, the

United States privately sought to encourage the Yeltsin government to avoid extralegal actions or steps that would restrict freedom of the press or civil liberties. Especially later in the 1990s, Clinton administration officials also raised concerns about official corruption, the rule of law, and freedom of the press in exchanges with senior Russian leaders. The American officials involved say these private entreaties contributed to President Yeltsin's decision at critical junctures to spurn the suggestion of some of his advisers to resort to extraconstitutional steps.[19]

Personal diplomacy at the top level is important on tough issues with strong domestic constituencies determined to block movement. Russia's movement toward deeper democracy is just such an issue.

In the 1990s, the emphasis on democratic values in America's Russia diplomacy was understandably circumscribed by the dominance of security issues left over from the Soviet era—such as facilitating the withdrawal back to Russia of strategic nuclear weapons in Ukraine and Belarus and the withdrawal of Russian conventional forces in the Baltic states. The United States also engaged cautiously on democracy issues when it was widely recognized that the possible return to power of a communist-led coalition with far less commitment to democracy than the Yeltsin government was a serious possibility. With the threat of a communist restoration declining and movement toward closer under-standing on many other fronts, democracy can and will move toward center stage in the relationship. Handling the issue effectively will require sustained personal diplomacy along with other diplomatic avenues.

In some respects, President Putin is a more promising partner for per-sonal diplomacy than former president Yeltsin. A product of the Soviet and Russian bureaucracy, Putin is both more accomplished at and more committed to seeing bilateral agreements through the Russian bureau-cratic labyrinth. His popularity, moreover, gives him clout within the system that President Yeltsin was not able to muster for most of his tenure, owing to the low esteem in which the Russian public held him. Recent polling indicates solid public backing for Putin's post–September

11 approach to relations with the United States and for his performance in office more generally.[20]

Establishing a strong and productive personal relationship at the top level is not the same thing as identifying American policy with the Russian president or other individual leaders. Presidents George H. W. Bush and Bill Clinton, in the late 1980s and early 1990s, faced a highly polarized political environment. At the time Soviet leader Gorbachev and President Yeltsin faced internal opposition determined to scuttle liberalizing reforms. In that context, the U.S. government sought to maintain contacts with a spectrum of Russian political actors but at the same time aligned American policy closely and explicitly with Gorbachev and then Yeltsin and against their political opponents. Former secretary of state Warren Christopher documents the early efforts of the Clinton administration to provide direct U.S. backing for President Yeltsin and "Russia's democrats."[21]

The administration timed many of its pronouncements and summit meetings to give a political boost to Yeltsin and his government in their political battle with internal opponents. This policy reached a climax when Yeltsin acted outside the constitution in October 1993 to disband the parliament in order to propose a new constitution and schedule new elections. The administration publicly backed Yeltsin's actions, concluding that the opposition was opposed to democracy and market reform and prepared to use extraconstitutional means in their own right were they to take charge.[22]

Critics of American policy in this era argue that, under Gorbachev and under Yeltsin, American policy became too closely identified with the top leader and his policies and insufficiently critical of policies that were potentially antidemocratic. The record suggests that the close relationships American leaders developed with Gorbachev and then Yeltsin did not prevent them from pressing the two leaders to stay on a democratic course or criticizing actions that were seen as antidemocratic. But the decision to associate the United States closely with two leaders who ultimately proved highly unpopular contributed to the turn toward skepticism about American intentions and American advice during the 1990s. It is not clear, moreover, that explicit support for individual leaders contributed any more to encouraging Russia's movement along a democratic path than strong backing for democratic principles alone would have accomplished.

Focusing on the Power of Political Opposition and a Free Press

The greatest single obstacle to Russia's movement toward deeper democracy is the lack of a strong political opposition capable of challenging current policies and entrenched privileges without fear of retribution. Creating an institutional framework where opposition can flourish is the Russian leadership's responsibility.

A press independent of state influence, experience in many countries suggests, is also the core freedom that works to protect and expand other democratic freedoms and serves as a check on the state and vested private interests. A free press is essential if Russia is to have the kind of open debate about democratic values necessary to reach a national consensus on a way forward compatible with Russian history and political culture.

The challenges to a free press from central and some regional governments in Russia in the Putin era have made defending freedom of the press the top priority for Russia's proponents of faster movement toward democracy. For the same reasons encouraging policies that facilitate the creation of an unfettered press should be at the top of the list for American leaders as they engage Russian officials on the way forward to closer integration with Western institutions. The U.S. and Russian governments, recognizing the importance that press freedom is assuming in the U.S.-Russian relationship, in late 2001 facilitated the creation of the Russian-American Media Entrepreneurship Dialogue, a forum led by nongovernment organizations designed to advance the objective of strengthening the economic foundations for a Russian independent press.[23]

The media dialogue about financial independence is a good first step necessary for ongoing dialogue. But the obstacles to an unfettered press in Russia are as much political as economic. A solid financial footing is key to media independence in the long run, but in the short run the route to an unfettered press and a competitive political marketplace depends more on the policies of the Putin administration and the Russian government than on the ups and downs of newspaper subscriptions and advertising budgets. The Russian-American dialogue should have a political as well as an economic component. The presidential administrations in both countries can achieve this goal by helping to create a forum that brings together media leaders, journalists, and government officials to discuss the overtly political issues of ownership, government policy, and government-media relations

The War in Chechnya: Challenge to Russian Democracy

From 1994 to 1996 and again since 1999, Russian military and security services have been engaged in a prolonged and costly war against insurgents in the Russian region of Chechnya fighting for independence from Russia. While fighting for its territorial integrity and against insurgents, some of whom have no compunction about using terror, Russia's conduct of the war has featured recurring and serious violations of human rights. UN, European, Russian, American, and nongovernmental organizations have documented numerous extralegal killings, indiscriminate use of force against noncombatants, torture, unexplained disappearances of Chechen citizens, and other violations of Russian and international law.[24]

Those who monitor the war in Chechnya are concerned not only by the persistent reports of human rights violations but also by the failure of the Russian government to follow up such reports and successfully prosecute offenders from the Russian forces. The failure to prosecute offenders is not a matter of insufficient legislation. Besides laws already on the books, military authorities have responded to complaints from domestic and international groups by issuing decrees that seek to enforce discipline, require closer oversight of operations by civilian prosecutors and other government authorities, and improve the public's ability to seek redress of grievances. The problem, according to Russian and international observers, is that these legal regulations are rarely implemented.

The war in Chechnya and Russian attitudes toward it symbolize and embody the contradictory currents shaping Russian democracy today. On the one hand, Russian human rights organizations are among the most vigorous of those seeking to limit abuses by Russian forces and demanding that the government investigate reports of human rights violations. The Russian government has issued new laws and regulations that suggest a sincere intent to limit abuses and make it easier for victims to seek redress.

On the other hand, the government in general—and the military hierarchy in particular—has shown itself unable to marshal the commitment or capability to act on its promises to limit human rights abuses or to implement its decrees designed to achieve those objectives. As on other issues critical to Russia's advance toward deeper democracy, President Putin's rhetoric about human rights in Chechnya has not been matched by action.

Restrictions on the ability of the Russian press to investigate and expose official malfeasance are an important factor impeding reduction of human rights abuses in Chechnya just as they impede Russia's democratic development more generally. Military and security authorities have prevented unfavorable stories of the war from seeing the light of day and have harassed Russian journalists who seek to investigate charges of abuses by Chechen families. American scholars who have studied the war conclude that the lack of press coverage is one reason for the lack of public reaction to reports of human rights abuses and the ability of elements of the military and security services to ignore legal provisions designed to restrict abuses.[25]

American leaders have expressed concern about human rights abuses in Chechnya and sought to encourage stronger safeguards since the early stages of the first conflict in the mid-1990s. Their entreaties have been tempered by the priority accorded other issues in the bilateral relationship, by a judgment that Chechnya is an internal issue, and by a recognition that some in the multifaceted resistance that Russia faces have been prepared to use brutal tactics and terror in their own right. As democracy issues loom larger in the U.S.-Russian relationship, American leaders should press for more vigorous efforts to control abuses by Russian forces in Chechnya. American and other international efforts will encourage those inside Russia who seek the same goal. More vigorous prosecution of reports of abuses will be a litmus test of Russia's progress toward deeper democracy.

U.S. Policies Make a Difference

The results of the past decade have given Americans and Russians a new appreciation of how long the creation of new political institutions can take. Formal structures and good legislation can lay the groundwork, but filling them with content is a gradual, incremental process. Bold leadership from the top was critical in the first stages of Russia's effort to create a new, more democratic order. It remains an essential ingredient to move Russia toward deeper democracy.

Creating new momentum is primarily a matter for Russia's citizenry and leadership. But U.S. efforts loom large in Russia's political debate, and U.S. policies make a difference, for better or for worse. How Russia chooses to move toward deeper democracy is for Russia's citizens to decide, but whether Russia succeeds in building a stronger democracy is a vital U.S. concern. Russia's success will require difficult decisions in Moscow, but it demands a deliberate strategy, high priority, and sustained engagement by American policymakers.

Notes

Chapter 1

1. Michael McFaul and Nikolai Zlobin, "A Half-Democratic Russia Will Always Be a Half-Ally of the United States," *Demokratizatsiya*, vol. 9 (Fall 2001), pp. 476–81.

2. Robert V. Daniels, "Russia's Democratic Dictatorship," *Dissent*, vol. 47 (Summer 2000); Stefan Hedlund, "Will the Russian Economy Revive under Putin?" *Problems of Post-Communism*, vol. 48 (March–April 2001), pp. 54–62.

3. By *democracy*, I mean in this book what academic scholars usually characterize as *liberal democracy*. Individual definitions vary in specifics, but most students of democracy emphasize in common that liberal democracy entails not only (1) free and competitive multicandidate elections, but also (2) strong protections for individual liberties and (3) a rule of law in which laws are transparent and are binding on all, including not just the citizens but the state itself. This is Marc Plattner's summary definition of liberal democracy in "Liberalism and Democracy: Can't Have One without the Other," *Foreign Affairs*, vol. 77, no. 2 (1998), p. 171. See also Larry Diamond, *Developing Democracy: Toward Consolidation* (Johns Hopkins University Press, 1999), pp. 10–13, and Robert Dahl,

Polyarchy, Participation, and Opposition (Yale University Press, 1971), pp. 5–8. I avoid the term *liberal democracy* because of its different, more partisan meaning in the American political context.

4. Stephen Holmes, *Passions and Constraint: On the Theory of Liberal Democracy* (University of Chicago Press, 1995), p. 19.

5. Michael E. Brown, Sean M. Lynn-Jones, and Steven E. Miller, eds., *Debating the Democratic Peace: An International Security Reader* (MIT Press, 1996); Spencer R. Weart, *Never at War: Why Democracies Will Not Fight One Another* (Yale University Press, 1998); Robert Jervis, "Theories of War in an Era of Leading-Power Peace," *American Political Science Review*, vol. 96 (March 2002), pp. 4–5. Edward D. Mansfield and Jack Snyder, "Democratization and the Danger of War," *International Security*, vol. 20 (Summer 1995), pp. 5–38, make the case that countries *in transition* to democracy become more war prone, not less.

6. Larry Diamond, "Is Pakistan the (Reverse) Wave of the Future?" *Journal of Democracy*, vol. 11 (July 2000), pp. 96–97; Samuel Huntington, *The Third Wave: Democratization in the Late Twentieth Century* (University of Oklahoma Press, 1991), p. 293.

Chapter 2

1. Quoted in "Two Years at the Helm," *Obshchaya Gazeta*, no. 2 (January 2002).

2. Richard Rose, "Russia Elects a President," *New Russia Barometer IX* (Glasgow: University of Strathclyde, Centre for the Study of Public Policy), p. 33; William Zimmerman, *The Russian People and Foreign Policy: Elite and Mass Perspectives, 1993–2000* (Princeton University Press, 2002), p. 7; Timothy J. Colton and Michael McFaul, "Are Russians Democratic?" Working paper 20 (Washington: Carnegie Endowment for International Peace, June 2001), pp. 7–8.

3. The 1999 poll is reported in United States Information Agency (USIA), "Opinion Analysis," M-27-99 (February 11, 1999), p. 4. In a 1997 survey, 87 percent of respondents chose "honest elections held regularly" as one of the features of the society in which they would like to live (USIA, "Opinion Analysis," M-70-97, May 1, 1997, p. 2).

4. Survey results on extending the president's term and on the preferred means for selecting regional governors were posted by the Public Opinion Foundation on its website (www.fom.ru) in March and May 2000, respectively.

5. Public opinion survey by the All-Russian Center for the Study of Public Opinion (hereafter, Vtsiom), posted at www.polit.ru in July 2000.

6. The polling data cited here regarding views on freedom of the press are drawn from polls conducted by Vtsiom and posted at www.polit.ru in July 2000

and January 2001; and from a poll conducted by the Public Opinion Foundation and posted at http://english.fom.ru/reports/ in June 2000.

7. Radio Free Europe/Radio Liberty, *RFE/RL Security Watch*, vol. 2, no. 14 (April 9, 2001); Vtsiom, posted at www.polit.ru in November 2000; Department of State, Office of Research Opinion Analysis, "Russian Journalists and Public Don't See Eye-to-Eye on Threats to Free Speech," M-96-01 (April 25, 2001).

8. Robert V. Daniels, "Putting Putin to the Test," *New Leader*, vol. 84 (September–October 2000), pp. 11–13; Alexander Lukin, "Electoral Democracy or Electoral Clanism? Russian Democratization and Theories of Transition," *Demokratizatsiya* (Winter 1999), p. 97.

9. To a degree, popular support for restraints on presidential power is dependent on popular attitudes toward the incumbent president. Recent polls show that since the replacement of former President Yeltsin—highly unpopular at the end of his term—by Vladimir Putin, support for the idea of giving the Duma wider authority to approve presidential appointees has declined somewhat. Other recent polling data indicate that many who support separation of powers in the abstract are at the same time prepared to support steps by Putin to increase his power at the expense of the Duma and the regional governors in the current political environment. Polling results relevant to the issue of separation of powers between the president and the Duma are presented in a survey posted by the Public Opinion Foundation at www.fom.ru/reports/b1/of001801.html on May 18, 2000; in a May 2000 survey by Vtsiom, posted at www.polit.ru; in USIA, "Opinion Analysis," M-158-99 (August 6, 1999); and in Richard Rose, "Boris Yeltsin Faces the Electorate: Findings from Opinion Polling Data," *Demokratizatsiya*, vol. 4 (Summer 1996), pp. 386–87.

10. Polling data on attitudes toward the idea of political opposition in the early 1990s are presented in USIA, "Russian Public Still Wrestling with Democracy," memorandum, March 25, 1993; recent data are available at www.nemtsov.ru, posted November 15, 2000; John F. Kennedy School of Government, Strengthening Democratic Institutions project, *Russia Watch*, no. 4 (December 2000), p. 3; and www.polit.ru/printable/412654.html, posted April 25, 2001.

11. May 2000 poll by the Russian firm Russian Public Opinion and Market Research (hereafter, ROMIR), posted at www.romir.ru.

12. Results of the survey of Putin voters are published in Colton and McFaul, "Are Russians Democratic?" pp. 19–20. A Vtsiom survey published at the time of Putin's election indicated that 55 percent of Russian citizens expected him to "respect individual rights and private life," while 20 percent expected "subordination of the individual to the interests of the state."

13. Assessments of individual public opinion polls about democratic values, or of a limited set of polls, are relatively plentiful in the scholarly literature. Assessments that seek to determine trends in public opinion over the decade of the 1990s are rare. See Zimmerman, *The Russian People and Foreign Policy*; James L. Gibson, "Changes in Russian Attitudes toward Democratic and Economic Reform: Results from a 1996–2000 Panel Survey," paper prepared for the annual meeting of the American Political Science Association, August 27, 2000; Elena Bashkirova, "Value Change and Survival of Democracy in Russia 1995-2000," ROMIR paper, available at www.romir.ru/eng/value-change.htm; Yuriy Levada, "Soviet Man Ten Years Later, 1989–1999," *Russian Social Science Review*, vol. 42 (January–February 2001), pp. 4–28.

14. Peter Reddaway and Dmitri Glinski, *The Tragedy of Russia's Reforms: Market Bolshevism against Democracy* (United States Institute of Peace Press, 2001), pp. 93–97; M. Steven Fish, *Democracy from Scratch* (Princeton University Press, 1995), p. 28.

15. The Communist Party received 12 percent of the vote in the 1993 elections for the State Duma, 22 percent in 1995, and 24 percent in 1999. Opinion polls indicate that 20–25 percent of potential voters still say that they would vote for the party if new elections were held. For a discussion of nationalist and other extremist groups, see Stephen D. Shenfield, *Russian Fascism: Traditions, Tendencies, Movements* (Armonk, N.Y.: M. E. Sharpe, 2001), esp. p. 262.

16. This summary of the democratic idea in pre-Soviet Russia is based on Richard Pipes, *Russia under the Old Regime* (Collier, 1992), esp. p. 112; Richard Pipes, *Property and Freedom* (Alfred A. Knopf, 1999), esp. pp. 204–08; George Fischer, *Russian Liberalism* (Harvard University Press, 1958), esp. p. 172; Richard Charques, *The Twilight of Imperial Russia* (Oxford University Press, 1965), esp. p. 40; Melissa Kirschke Stockdale, *Paul Miliukov and the Quest for a Liberal Russia, 1880–1918* (Cornell University Press, 1996), p. 164; Charles E. Timberlake, ed., *Essays on Russian Liberalism* (University of Missouri Press, 1972); Fiona Hill, "In Search of Great Russia," Ph.D. dissertation, Harvard University (March 1998), p. 448; and Jeffrey W. Hahn, *Regional Russia in Transition: Studies from Yaroslavl'* (Johns Hopkins University Press, 2001), chap. 4, who makes the case that Russian political culture has changed slowly over time as a result of education and modernization.

17. Donna Bahry, "Society Transformed? Rethinking the Social Roots of Perestroika," *Slavic Review*, vol. 52 (Fall 1993), pp. 512–54, provides an excellent overview of the data from émigré interviews as it pertains to democracy and political liberalization.

18. A recent survey of changing Russian attitudes toward market reforms over the last decade found that in 2001, 18 percent of respondents supported a "fully centralized management of the economy and price control," 37 percent supported a mixture of state sector and increased private sector opportunities, and 8 percent supported "maximum" freedom for the private sector. Reported in the Jamestown Foundation's *Russia and Eurasian Review*, vol. 1, no. 3 (July 2, 2002).

19. See, for instance, data from the 1995–98 World Values Survey reported in Ronald Inglehart, "Political Culture and Democratic Institutions: Russia in Global Perspective," paper presented to the annual meeting of the American Political Science Association, Washington, August 31–September 2, 2000, table 3.

20. Polling results on attitudes toward the political party system, other than those cited in the tables, are presented in Colton and McFaul, "Are Russians Democratic?" p. 12, and a Vtsiom poll posted at www.polit.ru on March 21, 2001.

21. For these USIA-sponsored polls, see USIA, "Russian Public Still Wrestling with Democracy," memorandum, March 25, 1993, and USIA, "Opinion Analysis," M-70-97 (May 1, 1997). These results are consistent with other polls showing that Russian citizens see battling corruption as a top policy priority.

22. Vladimir Shlapentok, *Johnson's Russia List* (www.cdi.org/russia, hereafter *JRL*) 5188, April 5, 2001, item 10; Yuri Fedorov, "Democratization and Globalization: The Case of Russia," Working Paper 13 (Washington: Carnegie Endowment for International Peace, May 2000), esp. pp. 12–18.

23. Judith S. Kullberg and William Zimmerman, *World Politics*, vol. 51 (April 1999), pp. 323–58; Arthur H. Miller, Vicki L. Hesli, and William M. Reisinger, "Conceptions of Democracy among Mass and Elite in Post-Soviet Societies," *British Journal of Political Science*, vol. 27, part 1 (January 1997), p. 157.

24. See also the distinct contrast between elite and popular views when asked whether, in May 2000, it was now necessary to concentrate power in the hands of one individual; *Vremya MN*, May 12, 2000, p. 3.

25. For a good overview of this dimension of Russian politics in the 1990s, see Thomas Graham, "From Oligarchy to Oligarchy: The Structure of Russia's Ruling Elite," *Demokratizatsiya*, vol. 7 (Summer 1999), p. 325; Donald N. Jensen, "How Russia Is Ruled—1998," *Demokratizatsiya*, vol. 7 (Summer 1999), p. 341; Hans-Henning Schroder, "Eltsin and the Oligarchs: The Role of Financial Groups in Russian Politics between 1993 and 1998," *Europe-Asia Studies*, vol. 51 (September 1999), pp. 957–88; Vladimir Brovkin, "Fragmentation of Authority and Privatization of the State," *Demokratizatsiya*, vol. 6 (Summer 1998), pp. 504–17; and Virginie Coulloudon, "Elite Groups in Russia," *Demokratizatsiya*, vol. 6 (Summer 1998), pp. 535–49.

26. Department of State, Office of Research, "Russia: Back to the Future," Opinion Analysis M-190-99 (October 22, 1999), p. 5.

27. Vtsiom poll, posted at www.polit.ru on February 1, 2001.

28. Peter Rutland, "Has Democracy Failed Russia?" *National Interest*, vol. 38 (Winter 1994–95), p. 5; George Breslauer and others, "Russia at the End of Yeltsin's Presidency," *Post-Soviet Affairs*, vol. 16 (January–March 2000), p. 4; Alexander Dallin, "Where Have All the Flowers Gone?" in Gail Lapidus, ed., *The New Russia: Troubled Transformation* (Boulder, Colo.: Westview, 1994), p. 250; Anders Aslund and Mikhail Dmitriev, "Economic Reform versus Rent-Seeking," in Anders Aslund and Martha Brill Olcott, eds., *Russia after Communism* (Washington: Carnegie Endowment for International Peace, 1999), p. 124.

29. Michael Urban, *The Rebirth of Politics in Russia* (Cambridge University Press, 1997), p. 266.

30. Breslauer and others, "Russia at the End of Yeltsin's Presidency," pp. 1–6; George Breslauer, *Evaluating Yeltsin as Leader* (Washington: National Council for Eurasian and East European Research, March 24, 1999); Thomas Remington, *Politics in Russia* (Longman, 1999), p. 239; Jerry F. Hough, *The Logic of Economic Reform in Russia* (Brookings, 2001), pp. 6, 239.

31. This case is made by Kathryn Stoner-Weiss, "The Limited Reach of Russia's Party System: Under-Institutionalization in Dual Transitions," unpublished, March 9, 2000, who examines the experience of Russia and other countries undergoing dual economic and political transitions.

32. Angela Stent and Lilia Shevtsova, "No Turning Back," *Foreign Policy*, vol. 103 (Summer 1996), p. 93, and Blair Ruble, "The City, Contested Identity, and Democratic Transitions," *Demokratizatsiya*, vol. 9 (Spring 2001), pp. 173–81, discuss the Soviet legacy. Michael McFaul and Sarah E. Mendelson, "Russian Democracy—A U.S. National Security Interest," *Demokratizatsiya*, vol. 8 (Summer 2000), p. 338, discuss the preference for "imposition" over negotiation in the way political conflicts were resolved in the Yeltsin era.

33. James L. Gibson, "The Struggle between Order and Liberty in Contemporary Russian Political Culture," *Australian Journal of Political Science*, vol. 32, no. 2 (1997), p. 287.

34. See Marcia Weigle's discussion of postcommunist civil society in Russia in *Russia's Liberal Project: State-Society Relations in the Transition from Communism* (Pennsylvania State University Press, 2000), esp. pp. 377–79.

35. These data are discussed in Inglehart, "Political Culture and Democratic Institutions."

Chapter 3

1. George W. Breslauer, *Gorbachev and Yeltsin as Leaders* (Cambridge University Press, 2002), p. 13.

2. Igor Bunin, Boris Makarenko, and Konstantin Roslavlev, "Analysts: Putin-Elite Honeymoon Coming to End," *Nezavisimaya Gazeta*, June 20, 2000, p. 8, also available in *Current Digest of the Post-Soviet Press*, vol. 52, no. 25 (July 19, 2000), p. 5; Yegor Gaidar, "Hero of the Day," NTV television program, December 21, 2000.

3. Thomas F. Remington, "Putin and the Duma," *Post-Soviet Affairs*, vol. 17, (October–December 2001), pp. 285–308, describes the Putin administration's "systematic effort to develop and enact legislation reflecting the policy proposals laid out in the president's messages," contrasting this pattern with that under former president Yeltsin. The Putin administration's policies on key elements of democratic change are discussed more fully in chapter 4.

4. Text is available on the website of the Security Council of the Russian Federation, translated in Foreign Broadcast Information Service (FBIS), CEP20000913000294, September 13, 2000. The U.S. government makes subscriptions to FBIS available through World News Connection on the web.

5. Russians from across the political spectrum would agree that the country needs a stronger party system. Russia's political landscape has featured a plethora of parties, most of which have suffered from limited membership, short life, and no presence outside a handful of large cities. The new law on parties is available on the website of the Central Election Commission of the Russian Federation, www.fci.ru.

6. On the role of the presidential representatives, see Andrey Yegorov, "Polpredy Sozdayut Regionalnuyu Oppozitsiyu," www.strana.ru, May 16, 2001; and "Latshyev Holds First Meeting of Political Council" in the EastWest Institute's *Russian Regional Report*, vol. 6, no. 14 (April 18, 2001). Putin's meeting with representatives of civil society and its implications are discussed in Tatyana Malkina, "Khod po Gorizontali," *Vremya Novostei*, no. 102, June 14, 2001; and also Georgiy Satarov, "The Dialogue Is Initiated and Will Be Continued: Why the President Is Concerned with Problems of Civil Society," *Rossiyskaya Gazeta*, June 16, 2001, also available from FBIS, CEP20010619000081. Joan Barth Urban posted a good summary of a subsequent discussion by particpants about the implications of the meeting in *JRL* 5324, June 27, 2001, item 11.

7. The president's speeches are archived at http://president.kremlin.ru. Two of his most important early programmatic addresses are "Russia at the Turn of the

Millennium," www.government.gov.ru/government/minister/article-vvpl_txt.
html; and the address to Russia's Federal Assembly in July 2000, http://president.kremlin.ru/events/42.html.

8. Yevgeniy Yasin, "The President's Dilemma," *Segodnya*, December 15, 2000,
p. 5, available in FBIS, CEP20001215000148; Archie Brown, "Reaffirmation of
Central State Power," *Post-Soviet Affairs*, vol. 17, no. 1 (2001), pp. 46–49; Yuri
Fedorov, "Democratization and Globalization: The Case of Russia," Working
Paper 13 (Washington: Carnegie Endowment for International Peace, May 2000),
p. 21; Thomas E. Graham Jr., "Putin's Russia," remarks prepared for Bank of Finland Institute for Economies in Transition, December 14, 2000.

9. *ITAR-TASS*, October 29, 2000, summarizes a platform statement by the
Unity party. See also remarks by party leader Shoygu in *Obshchaya Gazeta*,
December 7, 2000, available from FBIS, CEP2000120800034; and the party's website, www.edinstvo.ru.

10. Data from opinion surveys of the Unity Party's Duma deputies, which
suggest considerable diversity within the party, are presented in Thomas F. Remington, "Party Cohesion in the Russian State Duma," unpublished paper, January
29, 2001.

11. See the interview with the party's first deputy chairman, Valentin Kuptsov,
in "Oppozitsiyu Mozhet Sostavit' Tol'ko KPRF," *Nezavisimaya Gazeta*, April 14,
2001; and Anna Zakatnova, "Novaya Politicheskaya Strategiya KPRF," *Nezavisimaya Gazeta*, April 27, 2001. Joan Barth Urban, "Zyuganov's Communists at
Odds," *New Leader*, vol. 83 (September–October 2000), pp. 14–16, and Andrey
Fedorov, "KPRF v Postyel'tsinskuyu Epokhu," *Nezavisimaya Gazeta*, November
30, 2000, provide background on the Communist party's positions in the Putin
era. The party's website is www.cprf.ru.

12. Documents setting out the formal program of Yabloko and the Union of
Right Forces can be found on their websites, www.yabloko.ru and www.sps.ru,
respectively. Yabloko leader Grigoriy Yavlinskiy's article "Liberalizm Dlya Vsekh,"
Obshchaya Gazeta, 26, June 28, 2001, gives a good overview of his party's positions. The Union of Right Forces website also contains separate documents
setting out its positions on economic and foreign policy and its approach to the
policies of the Putin administration.

13. Yabloko's position on relations with the Putin administration was presented by Yavlinskiy in a speech to the Moscow Helsinki group on May 12, 2001;
see www.yabloko.ru. The Union of Right Forces position is discussed by Boris
Nemtsov (elected as party leader at the founding congress in May 2001) in "Glupo
Byt' v Glukhoi Oppozitsii," *Izvestiya*, December 18, 2000. See also Anna Zakatnova, "SPS Yedin v Chetyryokh Litsakh," *Nezavisimaya Gazeta*, December 20,

2000. Thomas F. Remington, "Putin and the Duma," *Post-Soviet Affairs,* vol. 17 (October–December 2001), pp. 285–308, provides an analysis of voting patterns on key legislation by the main parties in the Duma.

14. Independent Duma deputy Boris Reznik, a member of the Duma's anti-corruption commission, argues that so far there is only a "simulated" campaign against corruption, with no sign of interest in the issue on the part of the Presidential Administration; Reznik, "Russia's Unhappy Image," *Vremya MN,* July 18, 2001 (available in FBIS, CEP20010718000344).

15. Transparency International's 2001 Corruption Perceptions Index is available at www.transparency.org/cpi/2001/cpi2001.html.

16. These problems are well summarized in Harley Balzer, "Human Capital and Russian Security in the Twenty-First Century," in Andrew C. Kutchins, ed., *Russia after the Fall* (Washington: Carnegie Endowment for International Peace, September 2002).

17. Judith Thornton, "Are There Lessons for Russia and the Reforming Socialist Economies?" in Hyung-Ki Kim and others, eds., *The Japanese Civil Service and Economic Development* (Oxford: Clarendon Press, 1995), p. 83; M. Steven Fish, "The Dynamics of Democratic Erosion," in George Breslauer and others, *Postcommunism and the Theory of Democracy* (Princeton University Press, 2001), p. 95.

18. For Russians and Americans who make this point, see Irina Khakamada, "Sekret Russkogo Mayatnika," *Moskovskiy Komsomolets,* February 20, 2001; Viktor Pokhmelkin, "Predposlednaya Kaplya," *Itogi,* no. 8 (February 2001); interview with Aleksey Arbatov in *Figury i Litsa,* no. 12 (2001) in *JRL* 5335, July 4, 2001; M. Steven Fish, *Democracy from Scratch* (Princeton University Press, 1995), p. 227; and Stephen Hanson, "Can Putin Rebuild the Russian State?" *Security Dialogue,* vol. 32 (June 2001), p. 264. For a similar perspective from the European Bank for Reconstruction and Development, see Stefan Wagstyl, "EBRD Vows to Raise Democratic Standards among Client States," *Financial Times,* April 25, 2001, p. 10.

19. Yasin, "The President's Dilemma"; Igor Bunin, Boris Makarenko, and Aleksey Makarkin, "Strategiya Vtorogo Shaga," *Segodnya,* January 4, 2001, discuss the political and economic agendas of different groups within or close to the Putin administration and the tensions between them.

20. Sergey Kovalev, *Ekho Moskvy,* January 31, 2001 (as posted on www.duma-sps.ru, February 2, 2001), and Mikhail Berger, "Long Live the One Party State," *Novye Izvestiya,* April 18, 2001 (as published in *JRL* 5209, no. 3, April 18, 2001), discuss the relevance of political survival skills learned in the Soviet era to the current environment. This point is also made by Yavlinskiy, "Liberalizm Dlya Vsekh."

21. See, for instance, the year-end review of Putin's policy in "God pri Putine," *Kommersant-Vlast,* no. 51 (December 26, 2000); see also Aleksandr Budberg,

"Heading for a Crisis," *Moskovskiy Komsomolets*, February 22, 2001 (as published in *JRL* 5110, no. 2, February 22, 2001); Andrey Kolganov, "Can Russia Afford a New National Anthem?" *Jamestown Foundation Prism*, vol. 6, no. 12 (2000), reprinted in *JRL* 4701, December 21, 2000, item 10.

22. Richard Rose, Meil Munro, and Stephen White make the case that Putin's support is fragile on the basis of an analysis of public opinion polls during the 2000 presidential election; Rose, Munro, and White, "How Strong Is Vladimir Putin's Support?" *Post-Soviet Affairs*, vol. 16 (October–December 2000), pp. 287ff.

23. Breslauer, *Gorbachev and Yeltsin as Leaders*, p. 234.

24. Putin's election in March 2000 was facilitated by Yeltsin's early resignation from office, which prompted an early election that capitalized on Putin's strong popular support as Russian premier and on the lack of preparedness of his opponents in the race.

25. Interview with Alexander Yakovlev by Alexander Gubanov, *Versty*, no. 19 (2001), as published in *JRL* 5113, February 23, 2001, item 3.

26. Thomas E. Graham Jr., *Russia's Decline and Uncertain Recovery* (Washington: Carnegie Endowment for International Peace, 2002), pp. 47–54; Eugene Huskey, *Presidential Power in Russia* (Armonk, N.Y.: M. E. Sharpe, 1999), esp. pp. 11, 37, 41, 101; Richard Neustadt, *Presidential Power and the Modern Presidents: The Politics of Leadership from Roosevelt to Reagan* (Free Press, 1990), esp. p. ix; Peter Reddaway, "Will Putin Be Able to Consolidate Power?" *Post-Soviet Affairs*, vol. 17 (January–March 2001), p. 23.

27. Yevgeniy Yasin in *Vremya Novostei*, December 14, 2000, as published in *JRL* 4649, December 20, 2000.

Chapter 4

1. Moynihan in Alexander Stille, "An Old Key to Why Countries Get Rich," *Orlando Sentinel*, February 18, 2001, p. 11; and Huntington, "Democracy's Third Wave," in Larry Diamond and Marc F. Plattner, eds., *Global Resurgence of Democracy* (Johns Hopkins University Press, 1996), p. 24.

2. Larry Diamond, "Promoting Democracy in the 1990s: Actors, Issues, and Imperatives," Report to the Carnegie Commission on Preventing Deadly Conflict (Carnegie Corporation of New York, December 1995), p. 60; Samuel Huntington, "Democracy's Third Wave," in Diamond and Plattner, *Global Resurgence of Democracy*, pp. 21–25; and John Higley and Richard Gunther, eds., *Elites and Democratic Consolidation in Latin America and Southern Europe* (Cambridge University Press, 1992), pp. 392–93.

3. Eugene Huskey, *Presidential Power in Russia* (Armonk, N.Y.: M. E. Sharpe, 1999), p. 161. Kelly M. McMann and Nikolai V. Petrov, *Post-Soviet Geography and Economics*, vol. 41, no. 3 (2000), pp. 155–82, conclude from a survey of democracy across Russia's regions that there is a positive correlation between strong democratic leaders in a region and the development of viable democratic institutions.

4. Robert D. Putnam, *Bowling Alone: The Collapse and Revival of American Community* (Simon and Schuster, 2000). See also Putnam's comments in Diamond and Plattner, *Global Resurgence of Democracy*, pp. 301–02; and Marc Marje Howard, "The Weakness of Post-Communist Civil Society," *Journal of Democracy*, 13, no. 1 (January 2002), p. 157. Michael McFaul, "The Fourth Wave: Democracy and Dictatorship in the Post-Communist World," unpublished paper, Stanford University, discusses the role of leaders in efforts to move from dictatorships to democracy.

5. An excellent account of the evolution of executive-legislative relations in Russia and an assessment of the relative checks and balances between the two branches is provided by Thomas F. Remington, "The Evolution of Executive-Legislative Relations in Russia since 1993," *Slavic Review*, vol. 59 (Fall 2000), pp. 499–520, and by Steven S. Smith and Thomas F. Remington, *The Politics of Institutional Choice: The Formation of the Russian State Duma* (Princeton University Press, 2001). See also Robert Sharlet, "Russian Constitutional Change: Proposed Power-Sharing Models," in Roger Clark, Ferdinand Feldbrugge, and Stanislaw Pomorski, eds., *International and National Law in Russia and Eastern Europe* (Kluwer Law International, 2001), p. 361.

6. Igor Klyamkin and Lilia Shevtsova, *This Omnipotent and Impotent Government: The Evolution of the Political System in Post-Communist Russia* (Carnegie Moscow Center, 1999) , pp. 51–55; Igor Grankin, "The Special Powers of Russia's Parliament," *Demokratizatsiya*, vol. 9 (Winter 2001), pp. 26–43; and Fedor Burlatskiy, "Change of Elite: Putin on the Verge of Solving a Very Important Problem," *Nezavisimaya Gazeta*, March 13, 2001. In an interview with *Delovye Lyudi*, May 6, 2001, on the eve of his selection as leader of the Union of Right Forces, Boris Nemtsov indicated that his priority was to increase the oversight and investigatory authorities of the Duma, while indicating that in his view it would not be wise to tamper at this time with the institution of the presidency.

7. Yabloko leader Yavlinskiy, "Sovet Federatsii Dolzhen Formirovat'sya Na Vybornoi Osnove," *Rosbalt*, June 9, 2001 (www.yabloko.ru [June 15, 2001]); Federation Council chairman Stroev, "Stroyev Calls for Elected Federation Council," *ITAR-TASS*, May 29; and Ol'ga Tropkina, "Imya Novogo Spikera SF Izvestno," *Nezavisimaya Gazeta*, June 16, 2001.

8. Thomas F. Remington, "Party Cohesion in the Russian State Duma," unpublished paper, Emory University, January 29, 2001.

9. M. Steven Fish argues the link between superpresidentialism and corruption in Victoria E. Bonnell and George W. Breslauer, eds., *Russia in the New Century: Stability or Disorder?* (Westview Press, 2001), p. 27. George Breslauer indicates that Yeltsin's policy of undermining the credibility of the Duma as an oversight body gave government bureaucrats space to ignore or reinterpret his own decrees in George Breslauer, *Gorbachev and Yeltsin as Leaders* (Cambridge University Press, 2002), p. 310.

10. Peter H. Solomon Jr. and Todd Foglesong, "The Procuracy and the Courts in Russia: A New Relationship?" *East European Constitutional Review*, vol. 9 (Fall 2000).

11. Summaries of the complex package of legislation include Natalia Melnikova and others, *Vedemosti*, April 12, 2001, and interviews with working group chief Kozak in *Rossiyskaya Gazeta*, June 19, 2001 (www.strana.ru, February 8, 2001). An overview and assessment of the reform package as adopted in December 2001 is offered by Peter H. Solomon Jr., "Putin's Judicial Reform: Making Judges Accountable as Well as Independent," *East European Constitutional Review*, vol. 11 (Winter–Spring 2002).

12. Yabloko's perspective is at www.yabloko.ru, May 16, 2001; the Union of Right Forces' perspective is in Natalia Alekseyeva and Aleksandr Sadchikov, "V Gosdume Idyot 'Presentatsiya' Sudebnoi Reformy,'" *Izvestiya*, May 16, 2001. Remarks by the prosecutor general are reported in "Ot Chego Nezavisim Prokuror?" *Rossiyskaya Gazeta*, April 28, 2001; and an analysis of the resistance by Radio Free Europe/Radio Liberty (RFE/RL) is at *JRL* 5223, April 26, 2001, item 11.

13. See the interview with State Duma deputy Elena Mizulina, *Nezavisimaya Gazeta*, June 21, 2002.

14. According to the Justice Ministry, which will be in charge of overseeing the provisions of the new law on parties, as of 2001 there were 59 political parties, 35 political organizations, and 104 political movements in Russia registered with the state and authorized to compete in elections. See *JRL* 5356, July 20, 2001, item 8.

15. Michael McFaul, "Party Formation and Non-Formation in Russia," Working Paper 12 (Washington: Carnegie Endowment for International Peace, May 2000), provides an excellent overview of the status of the party system and the explanations that have been offered for it. Stephen E. Hansen, "Instrumental Democracy: The End of Ideology and the Decline of Russian Political Parties," unpublished manuscript, makes the case for the role of ideology. McFaul, as well as Huskey, *Presidential Power in Russia*, p. 220, make the case that leadership

decisions by Yeltsin and his team played an important role in the party system's travails.

16. Seymour Martin Lipset, "The Indispensability of Political Parties," *Journal of Democracy*, vol. 11 (January 2000), pp. 48–55; Michael McFaul, *Russia's Unfinished Revolution* (Cornell University Press, 2001), p. 313; and Larry Diamond, "Toward Democratic Consolidation," in Diamond and Plattner, *Global Resurgence of Democracy*, p. 238.

17. See the interview with Central Election Commission chief Veshnyakov in *Segodnya*, January 5, 2001. Boris Nadezhdin offers a conditional liberal endorsement of the law at the Union of Right Forces' website, www.duma-sps.ru (the party's web address at the time), July 11, 2001.

18. See *EastWest Institute Russian Regional Report*, vol. 6, no. 26, July 9, 2001; interview with Election Commission chief Veshnyakov, www.strana.ru, July 13, 2001; and an article on regional parties by Vladimir Gelman and Grigorii Golosov, "Regional Party System Formation in Russia: The Deviant Case of Sverdlovsk Oblast," in John Lowenhardt, ed., *Party Politics in Post-Communist Russia* (Frank Cass, 1998), p. 31. Party representation in regional legislatures is discussed by Kathryn Stoner-Weiss, "The Limited Reach of Russia's Party System," unpublished manuscript, Princeton University, March 2000.

19. Klyamkin and Shevtsova, *This Omnipotent and Impotent Government*, p. 40; support by a Kremlin-linked spokesman is in Andrey Yegorov www.strana.ru, May 16, 2001; remarks by the leader of the main propresidential party, United Russia, are reported at www.strana.ru, May 28, 2002.

20. Putin's remarks include his interview in *Izvestiya*, March 22, 2001 (and in www.strana.ru, March 6, 2001).

21. This judgment on the role of elections is from Michael McFaul and Sarah E. Mendelson, "Russian Democracy—A U.S. National Security Interest," *Demokratizatsiya*, vol. 8 (Summer 2000), p. 332. The description of the mind-set of the more conservative elements of the political elite is taken from a seminal analysis of Yeltsin-era politics by Thomas E. Graham Jr., "Russia's New Regime," in *Nezavisimaya Gazeta*, November 23, 1995.

22. Many international organizations have been involved in monitoring Russia's elections and commenting on the results, including the International Foundation for Election Systems (IFES), the Organization for Security and Cooperation in Europe (OSCE), the National Democratic Institute, and the International Republican Institute. The most comprehensive assessments of fairness and recommendations for additional steps to enhance fairness have been provided by IFES and OSCE. See Christian Nadeau, ed., *Parliamentary and Presidential Elections in Russia* (IFES, 2000), and OSCE, "Russian Federation Elections

to the State Duma," final report of the Office for Democratic Institutions and Human Rights (ODIHR), February 13, 2000. On the general criteria for free and fair elections, see Jorgen Elklit and Palle Svensson, "What Makes Elections Free and Fair," *Journal of Democracy*, vol. 8 (July 1997), pp. 32–46.

23. OSCE, "Russian Federation Elections to the State Duma," p. 36. The new legislation and its impact on the ability of regional governors to manipulate elections is summarized by Dmitriy Kamyshev, "Governors Left without Choices," in *Kommersant-Vlast*, June 4, 2002.

24. Ol'ga Tropkina, "TSIK Ob'yavlyaet Novye Pravila Igry," *Nezavisimaya Gazeta*, July 14, 2001. The assessment of Russian court decisions is in Nadeau, *Parliamentary and Presidential Elections in Russia*, pp. 124–26.

25. OSCE, "Russian Federation Elections to the State Duma," p. 33.

26. The government legislation and the views of several analysts on it are discussed in *Kommersant-Vlast*, no. 23 (2001). Some election monitoring groups and Central Election Commission officials believe that this problem calls for better self-regulation on the part of the journalistic community rather than new regulations from the government.

27. International experience in election monitoring is discussed in articles by Thomas Carothers, "The Observers Observed," and by Neil Nevitte and Santiago A. Canton, "The Role of Domestic Observers," in *Journal of Democracy*, vol. 8, no. 3.

28. OSCE, "Russian Federation Elections to the State Duma," p. 25. A good history of Russian domestic monitoring efforts and U.S. assistance to those efforts is provided by Sarah Mendelson, "Democracy Assistance and Political Transition in Russia," *International Security*, vol. 25 (Spring 2001), p. 68. Some estimates suggest that election-day monitors were present at only one-fifth of Russian polling stations in the 1995 State Duma elections, while the OSCE reported seeing representatives from political parties or independent candidates at 98 percent of the stations they visited in the 1999 Duma elections. U.S.-government-backed nongovernment organizations are providing technical assistance to a group of Russian NGOs in establishing a national election monitoring organization. There are apparently no plans at this time, or sufficient resources, to carry out a nationwide parallel vote count during the 2003 Duma or 2004 presidential elections. Information from interviews with National Democratic Institute officials, July 2001.

29. Yabloko's proposal is at www.yabloko.ru (July 7, 2001).

30. See Jonathan Fox, "Latin America's Emerging Local Politics," *Journal of Democracy*, vol. 5 (April 1994), pp. 105–13, discussing the Latin American experience. See also Robert D. Putnam, *Making Democracy Work: Civic Traditions in*

Modern Italy (Princeton University Press, 1993), pp. 185, 201–03; and Diamond, "Toward Democratic Consolidation," in Diamond and Plattner, *Global Resurgence of Democracy*, pp. 231–32. Putnam, *Bowling Alone*, concludes, based on a study of American experience, that "social capital" or citizen activism is best facilitated by decentralizing government authority as far as possible to the local level. Jeffrey W. Hahn, *Regional Russia in Transition: Studies from Yaroslavl'* (Johns Hopkins University Press, 2001), chap. 1, provides an excellent overview of the theoretical literature on the relationship between democracy at the national and local levels, beginning with John Stuart Mill.

31. Richard Rose, "Postcommunism and the Problem of Trust," in Diamond and Plattner, *Global Resurgence of Democracy*, p. 262.

32. Alfred B. Evans Jr., "Economic Resources and Political Power at the Local Level in Post-Soviet Russia," *Policy Studies Journal*, vol. 28, no. 1 (2000), pp. 114–33, provides an excellent short overview of the history of democratic local government under Soviet rule as well as under Yeltsin. See also John F. Young, "Parallel Patterns of Power? Local Government Reform in Late Imperial and Post-Soviet Russia," *Canadian Slavonic Papers*, vol. 42 (September 2000), pp. 269–94.

33. Evans, "Economic Resources and Political Power"; and Young, "Parallel Patterns of Power?"

34. *Vremya Novostei*, June 20, 2001. On democratic local government, see statements by Yabloko leader Mitrokhin at www.strana.ru, January 19, 2001; Union of Right Forces leader Gaidar in *Izvestiya*, January 17, 2001; and Union of Right Forces leader Mintz in *Nezavisimaya Gazeta*, February 21, 2001. See also comments by Duma speaker and Communist Party leader Seleznev at www.strana.ru, June 19, 2001.

35. Archie Brown, "Vladimir Putin and the Reaffirmation of Central State Power," *Post-Soviet Affairs*, vol. 17 (January–March 2001), pp. 50–51; Peter Reddaway, "Will Putin Be Able to Consolidate Power?" *Post-Soviet Affairs*, vol. 17 (January–March 2001), pp. 32–33; Emil Pain, "New Trends in Federal and Nationalities Policy in Russia: From Yeltsin to Putin," paper prepared for the conference Russia—Ten Years After, sponsored by the Carnegie Endowment for International Peace, 2001; president of the Russian Congress of Municipal Organizations, Oleg Sysuyev, *Izvestiya*, June 20, 2001.

36. Putin's recent comments on local government can be found at www.polit.ru, April 3, 2001 (text of his April 3 statement to the Federal Assembly) and www.presscenter.ru, February 20, 2001 (remarks to a group of regional governors).

37. See Young, "Parallel Patterns of Power?" p. 291.

38. Ken Rogerson, "The Role of Media in Transitions from Authoritarian Systems: Russia and Poland since the Fall of Communism," *East European Quarterly*, vol. 31 (Fall 1997), pp. 329–53.

39. "Each person has the right freely to seek, receive, pass on, produce, and disseminate information by any legal method." Excerpt from article 29 of the 1993 Russian constitution.

40. Nicholas Daniloff discusses the press law in "Will Russia's Free Press Survive?" *Fletcher Forum of World Affairs*, vol. 17 (Winter 1993), pp. 35–48. According to some estimates, by 1999 out of a total of around 12,000 print publications, 2,140 were state owned. There were approximately 800 television channels, of which 500 were privately owned. See European Institute for the Media, *Media in the CIS* (1999).

41. This estimate is provided by Fedor Burlatskiy in *Nezavisimaya Gazeta*, March 13, 2001, available in *JRL* 5175, March 29, 2001. According to some estimates, Russia's television advertising market dropped from around $550 million in 1997 to less than $200 million in 1999. See Celestine Bohlen, "The Unique Evolution of Russian TV," *New York Times*, April 29, 2001, p. 4, and Jeanne Whalen, "Despite the TV Fire, Russian Ad Sales Are Strong," *Wall Street Journal*, September 11, 2000.

42. Among the most important organizations monitoring the freedom of the press in Russia are Glasnost Defense Fund (www.gdf.ru), the European Institute for the Media (www.eim.org), Internews Russia (www.internews.ru), and the Moscow Media Law and Policy Center (www.medialaw.ru).

43. The Union of Right Forces' four-point proposal is available at www.nemtsov.ru, April 16, 2001. The proposal by Sergey Kashin for an independent press regulatory agency is available at www.strana.ru, April 11, 2001.

Chapter 5

1. James A. Baker III, *The Politics of Diplomacy: Revolution, War, and Peace 1989–1992* (G. P. Putnam's Sons, 1995), p. 568.

2. Larry Diamond, "Promoting Democracy," *Foreign Policy*, vol. 87 (Summer 1992), pp. 25–46; and Morton H. Halperin, "Guaranteeing Democracy," *Foreign Policy*, vol. 91 (Summer 1993), pp. 105–22.

3. The account in this chapter of the history of U.S. engagement with Soviet and Russian leaders on human rights and democracy issues is based in part on the memoirs of former national security adviser Zbigniew Brzezinski, former secretary of state George Shultz, former president George Bush, former national security adviser Brent Scowcroft, former secretary of state James Baker, former

secretary of state Warren Christopher, former deputy secretary of state Strobe Talbott, former U.S. ambassador to the USSR Jack Matlock, and former director of Central Intelligence and deputy national security adviser Robert Gates, as well as on interviews with former U.S. ambassador to Russia Thomas Pickering and other former U.S. officials and U.S. analysts of Russian affairs: Warren Christopher, *In the Stream of History: Shaping Foreign Policy for a New Era* (Stanford University Press, 1998); Strobe Talbott, *The Russia Hand: A Memoir of Presidential Diplomacy* (Random House, 2002); Baker III, *The Politics of Diplomacy*; Jack F. Matlock Jr., *Autopsy on an Empire: The American Ambassador's Account of the Collapse of the Soviet Union* (Random House, 1995); George H. W. Bush and Brent Scowcroft, *A World Transformed* (Alfred A. Knopf, 1998); George P. Shultz, *Turmoil and Triumph: My Years as Secretary of State* (Charles Scribner's Sons, 1993); and Robert M. Gates, *From the Shadows: The Ultimate Insider's Story of Five Presidents and How They Won the Cold War* (Simon and Schuster, 1996).

4. Shultz, *Turmoil and Triumph*, p. 122.

5. Baker, *The Politics of Diplomacy*, p. 65.

6. Poll results published in U.S. Department of State, Office of Research, "Russia's Mistrust of the U.S. at New High," Opinion Analysis M-30-00, March 14, 2000; Vtsiom poll, www.wciom.ru, May 2000; and Vtsiom poll, www.polit.ru, July 20, 2001.

7. Results of a poll sponsored by the U.S. Information Agency of Russian adults in December 1991 on the eve of the USSR's collapse; USIA memorandum, January 21, 1992.

8. Jack Matlock Jr., "Dealing with a Russia in Turmoil," *Foreign Affairs*, vol. 75 (May–June 1996), p. 49; Angela Stent and Lilia Shevtsova, "No Turning Back," *Foreign Policy*, vol. 103 (Summer 1996), pp. 102–03; Bill Bradley, "Eurasia Letter: A Misguided Russia Policy," *Foreign Policy*, vol. 101 (Winter 1995–96), pp. 83–84; George Breslauer, *Gorbachev and Yeltsin as Leaders* (Cambridge University Press, 2002), p. 191. Zbigniew Brzezinski argued the case for NATO enlargement as "insurance" against negative outcomes in Russia in "The Premature Partnership," *Foreign Affairs*, vol. 73 (March–April 1994), pp. 67–82.

9. See Clifford Gaddy and Fiona Hill, "Putin's Agenda, America's Choice: Russia's Search for Strategic Stability," Policy Brief 99 (Brookings, May 2002).

10. Aleksey Arbatov, Duma deputy from Yabloko, "Russia and NATO–Ten Years After," paper prepared for the Carnegie conference Russia—Ten Years After, June 8–10, 2001.

11. Stephen E. Hansen, "Defining Democratic Consolidation," in Richard D. Anderson Jr. and others, *Postcommunism and the Theory of Democracy* (Princeton University Press, 2001), p. 145.

12. Ira Strauss, "Russia's Potential Futures in the Euro-Atlantic World," *Demokratizatsiya*, vol. 9 (Fall 2001), pp. 485–97, provides a good overview of Russia's status and prospects in important Western institutions. Zbigniew Brzezinski, "Living with Russia,'" *National Interest* (Fall 2000), pp. 5–16, suggests that both NATO and the EU, perhaps jointly, issue formal statements supporting Russia's inclusion. Other proposals for Russia's inclusion include Fareed Zakaria, "Could Russia Join the West?" *Newsweek International*, June 25, 2001; James Chace and Charles Kupchan, "Bring Mother Russia into the Fold," *Los Angeles Times*, July 1, 2001, p. 5; Timothy Garton Ash, "Russia's Eventual Place in NATO," *New York Times*, July 23, 2001; and former Russian ambassador to the United States Vladimir Lukin, *Interfax*, July 2, 2001, as published in *JRL* 5333, July 3, 2001.

13. A fact sheet on the council can be found at www.state.gov/p/eur/rls/fs/10517.htm.

14. See reported remarks of former Russian National Security Council chief Ivan Rybkin in a UPI report published in *JRL* 6288, no. 11, June 4, 2002. See also Istvan Gyarmati and Christopher Walker, "Reconceptualizing NATO," *EastWest Institute Policy Brief* (http://psp.iews.org.).

15. This was just as true in the Soviet era. Proponents of liberalization told American diplomats that President Ronald Reagan's public comments about the "evil empire" galvanized their activity in the 1980s. Andrey Sakharov told Ambassador Matlock that it was important to keep pressure on Gorbachev as well as to applaud his steps in the right direction. Matlock argues that the United States could have done more than it did to put pressure on Gorbachev to back a plan for movement toward market reform prepared by his advisers in 1991; Matlock, *Autopsy on an Empire*, p. 589. See also remarks by prodemocratic Russian officials cited by Talbott in *The Russia Hand*, p. 41.

16. The statement by the association, including former officials such as Mikhail Gorbachev and Andrey Kokoshin, was reported in *Dipkurier NG*, no. 8, 2001, reproduced in *JRL* 5283, item 11, June 5, 2001.

17. Former secretary of state Shultz explicitly opposed such formal linkage although he suggests others in the Reagan administration were more sympathetic. Ambassador Matlock suggests that there was no formal linkage made between human rights and other issues in the late 1980s, but that it was clear to Soviet leaders that failure to deal with one issue on the agenda would affect progress on the others. See Matlock, *Autopsy on an Empire*, p. 85.

18. Remarks at the Carnegie Foundation, June 6, 2002.

19. Christopher, *In the Stream of History*, pp. 47, 101; and interview with Thomas Pickering, U.S. ambassador to Moscow from 1993 to 1996.

20. In a late May 2002 poll by the Russian organization Vtsiom, Putin drew favorable ratings for achieving "mutual concessions" in negotiations with the United States in comparison to "one-sided concessions" that large numbers of respondents attributed to former leaders Gorbachev and Yeltsin.

21. Christopher, *In the Stream of History.*

22. Secretary of State Christopher explained this policy in an October 23, 1993, speech in Moscow just after the events; Christopher, *In the Stream of History*, p. 97. A critical view of the administration's actions is in Peter Reddaway, *The Tragedy of Russia's Reforms* (Washington: U.S. Institute of Peace), chap. 7.

23. Details of the dialogue can be found on www.internews.ru.

24. See the U.S. Department of State's *Human Rights Report* for 2001, released in 2002 (www.state.gov/g/drl/rls/hrrpt/2001).

25. Theodore P. Gerber and Sarah E. Mendelson, "The Disconnect in How Russians Think about Human Rights and Chechnya: A Consequence of Media Manipulation," PONARS Policy Memo 244.

Index